Dynamic Teachers

This book is dedicated, with great love, to our children—Bethany; Dara and Tamara; David; and Lucy, Carolyn, and Valerie—from whom we have learned vital lessons about teaching and learning. For them, and for all children, we hope this book makes a small difference.

Dynamic Teachers

Leaders of Change

**Sharon F. Rallis and
Gretchen B. Rossman
with Janet M. Phlegar
and Ann Abeille**

CORWIN PRESS, INC.
A Sage Publications Company
Thousand Oaks, California

For information address:

Corwin Press, Inc.
A Sage Publications Company
2455 Teller Road
Thousand Oaks, California 91320

SAGE Publications Ltd.
6 Bonhill Street
London EC2A 4PU
United Kingdom

SAGE Publications India Pvt. Ltd.
M-32 Market
Greater Kailash I
New Delhi 110 048 India

Printed in the United States of America

Library of Congress Cataloging-in-Publication Data

Main entry under title:

Dynamic teachers: Leaders of change / Sharon F. Rallis . . . [et al.].
   p. cm.
   Includes bibliographical references (p.   ) and index.
   ISBN 0-8039-6235-5 (cloth: alk. paper). — ISBN 0-8039-6236-3 (pbk.: alk. paper)
   1. Teachers—United States. I. Rallis, Sharon F.
LB1775.2.D95 1995
371.1′02—dc20   95-15691

This book is printed on acid-free paper.

95 96 97 98 99 10 9 8 7 6 5 4 3 2 1

Sage Production Editor: Diana E. Axelsen

Contents

Foreword

As a teacher, I do not have to look far to find the six principles, the seven tenets, the nine steps, the three pillars, and so forth, of school reform. But I am often left wondering how they apply to John's problem in reading; to Sonya's need for more of a challenge in math; to a class in which more than half the children do not speak English; or to a class in which 65% of students who start the year do not finish it. The principles of school reform always sound good, but teachers are left wondering what they would look like in *our* classrooms. We wonder what would have to change in order to implement these principles with *our* children.

As classroom teachers, we often feel we lack the power or position to change organizational structures, curriculum requirements, or educational legislation. But there is one place we can all begin to have a huge impact on improving education for our children in the 21st century. This change begins with our own image of what it means to be a teacher.

Rallis and Rossman give us a unique insight into the complex thoughts, feelings, and actions of the teacher who is committed to making education work for all children in his or her classroom, school, and community. We get to know Don and Maggie, who are not actual people but composites of the qualities that define the principles and attitudes a teacher must have to succeed in our classrooms today. We get a glimpse into the thoughts and feelings of the teachers who will stop at nothing to make education work for *all* children. They are described with great sensitivity and insight into the multiple roles and many levels on which a teacher must operate to met the academic and social needs of the children.

The beginning teacher will be inspired by the models of excellence that are so thoroughly portrayed. These are examples that give a very practical and concrete guide to what it means to be a teacher. Those with more experience will be challenged by the depth and breadth of thought these exemplary teachers devote to every aspect of their work. There isn't a teacher in a classroom today who will not find some idea in this book that will push, stretch, or challenge him or her to deepen or extend thinking and practice.

We meet teachers in this book who are dealing with the realities of teaching in many of our school today. Rallis et al. do not give us two-dimensional teachers, cut out from an ideal but unrealistic world. Don and Maggie demonstrate the joys and delights of our profession, but no less the deep frustrations born of the innumerable obstacles that work against our success.

As we get to know Don and Maggie, we get a glimpse of what it means to be a teacher preparing our children for a new generation. They become not only practical models but also familiar friends who will inspire the thoughts, feelings, and actions that our profession demands from those who will lead our children into a new century.

STEVEN LEVY
1992-1993 Massachusetts
Teacher of the Year
Lexington, Massachusetts

Preface

The context of schools is changing because the world is changing. New forces are affecting schools, bringing new demands and challenges. In *Principals of Dynamic Schools: Taking Charge of Change,* a book that looks at principals in schools that have chosen to change, Goldring and Rallis (1993) ask, What are principals doing differently to deal with the new forces affecting their schools? Goldring and Rallis describe a new kind of principal who responds proactively to these forces. These principals have adopted new roles in response to these forces. Our book, *Dynamic Teachers: Leaders of Change,* is motivated by similar questions about teachers: How are teachers responding to the new forces affecting schools and classrooms? What are teachers who have chosen to respond proactively to the new challenges doing differently? What new roles are they adopting to deal with the new forces in the classroom?

Daily, teachers embark on varied paths to ensure that children will learn. They face classrooms that reflect a changing society. Many classrooms are exciting places where children interact with information, people, and objects in activities that enable them to shape deeper, more complex, and more useful understandings of the changing world. At the same time, other classrooms remain mere holding tanks where children memorize information to meet irrelevant requirements from an old world. *Dynamic Teachers* is about teachers who create and support learner-centered classrooms, where children's individual needs and abilities are recognized and nurtured to prepare them to succeed in a changing world.

Most teachers are doing their best to meet the needs of their students, struggling with the realities of today's classrooms and communities. Among them, however, a new type of teacher is emerging. These teachers are creating classroom communities that are truly focused on learning and building knowledge, rather than on merely transmitting information. The work of these teachers stands out because it reveals new roles they have adopted to meet the challenges they face. Through these new roles, they are beginning to achieve the goal of helping children think and learn, of preparing them for the unknown challenges that lie in their futures. We call these teachers "dynamic teachers." This book introduces Maggie and Don, two of the many dynamic teachers who are transforming schools today.

Our purpose in *Dynamic Teachers* is to provide a portrait of the emerging dynamic teacher, illustrating in concrete ways how these educators differ from their colleagues and highlighting the reasons why such differences are essential to the success of schooling in the future. We have written this book because we are committed to improving the lives of all children through education and because we have seen the teachers we describe throughout this book, the Maggies and the Dons, make a difference—to our children and to our future.

Dynamic Teachers is about teachers who value the rights of children and act on their beliefs in creative and effective ways to ensure that their students build useful understandings of their worlds. These teachers are not unique to the "best of the best" schools or the wealthiest schools or the most innovative schools or any other particular type of school. They can be found in any school. Many factors influence the effectiveness of an educator—educational preparation and training, financial resources, community support, school culture and organization, leadership, professional development opportunities; the list is enormous. But regardless of the school reality, any teacher can take on some, if not all, of the new roles of the dynamic teacher. If there is a message in *Dynamic Teachers*, it is that teachers can and do make a difference, and that the roles they assume in order to make that difference are becoming increasingly clear. We hope that educators, policymakers, parents, and community members will find something in *Dynamic Teachers* that helps them be more effective as educators or as advocates of teachers striving to create learner-centered school communities.

Overview of the Book

In the chapters that follow, we describe and explore seven emerging roles that, taken together, form what we call the "dynamic teacher." The roles are interactive and overlapping, though we have attempted here to make the distinctions as clear as possible to reinforce the essence of each role. Certain roles stand out within particular contexts and at different times in individual careers. Few educators are exemplary in all these roles—but we maintain that the more teachers can develop expertise in each of the roles, the more effective they will be in educating children, given the realities they—and we—confront. A dynamic teacher is

a moral steward;
a constructor;
a philosopher;
a facilitator;
an inquirer;
a bridger; and
a changemaker.

Chapter 1 introduces the dynamic teacher and some characteristics common to dynamic teachers we have seen. The chapter also examines the forces that create the need for the new roles required to meet the demands and challenges of today's classroom:

- Student bodies today are more diverse with varied needs.
- Parents and community groups have more influence on the school.
- The social, economic, and technological needs of the workplace place new demands on workers.
- Public demand for results has produced federal and state mandates and an overabundance of special programs.
- General acceptance of the status quo in education creates barriers to improvement.

Chapters 2, 3, and 4 examine the qualities with which the dynamic teacher approaches the classroom; he or she is a moral steward, a constructor, a philosopher. Chapter 2 discusses the values that drive the actions of dynamic teachers, who believe that each child has the right to reach his or her potential to live a full life and that the purpose of education is to ensure that right. The teaching of dynamic teachers demonstrates their acceptance of the responsibilities accompanying that task.

Chapter 3 explores how dynamic teachers make sense of the subjects they teach, the craft of teaching, and the development of children. Dynamic teachers use their knowledge and skills to help children construct their own interpretations of experience and to test these constructs against existing culturally accepted interpretations.

Chapter 4 reveals how dynamic teachers use a philosophy of professional commitment to shape the experience of schooling for children. This philosophy is one of action, reflection, and accountability.

In Chapters 5, 6, 7, and 8, we develop the new roles the dynamic teacher adopts in the classroom. Chapter 5 introduces the *facilitator,* who enacts the learner-centered classroom where children integrate their own knowledge construction with that of their peers and with what has been accepted in the various content areas. The facilitator creates, questions, connects, and coordinates in a classroom quite different from the traditional classroom.

Chapter 6 presents dynamic teachers as *inquirers.* In this role, they ask critical questions about what their students should learn and have learned. They offer strategies for knowing what students are learning and for satisfying the numerous audiences also asking for evidence of learning.

In Chapter 7 we meet the *bridger,* the teacher who blurs the boundaries between the classroom and the communities that influence it. Dynamic teachers recognize that the classroom is not an island unto itself, so they work to develop a sense of community or relationship to the world in which the classroom is embedded. They draw resources from groups external to the classroom, and they orchestrate opportunities whereby the school can enrich the community.

Chapter 8 shows dynamic teachers as *changemakers.* They become leaders for change; they take charge of the environment, using forces to build better places for children to learn.

Each chapter follows a similar design. We introduce a scenario with Maggie Clark and Don Medeiros, dynamic teachers at the O'Henry School. In each scenario, Maggie and Don exemplify the role we portray in that chapter. We illustrate and validate the role characteristics through examples and supporting literature.

Knowledge Sources

The roles explicated in this book emerge from our work in and with schools that are choosing to transform. Maggie and Don are our creations, but their characters and actions are a composite of the many teachers we have observed who have contributed to our conceptualization of a dynamic teacher. This conceptualization is grounded in current thinking about teaching and learning, school change, and organizations, and in what we've learned from our work with teachers. We bring wide experience to the writing of this book, from teaching at all levels (elementary to college), to policy making as a school board member. We all share, in some way, involvement with the Designing Schools for Enhanced Learning project (see Appendix A), an initiative of the Regional Laboratory for Educational Improvement of the Northeast and Islands. Sharon F. Rallis coordinates the project; Gretchen B. Rossman conducts the external evaluation; Janet M. Phlegar was one of the designers of the initiative and is the overall director of the Laboratory's programs; and Ann Abeille is the internal evaluator. Our work with this project, which includes a network of schools choosing to become more learner centered and inquiry oriented, provided the original inspiration for this book. The majority of our examples are drawn from teachers we have seen in these schools.

Through this school transformation network and its evaluation, we have amassed data on teachers who are proactively and successfully meeting the challenges of today's classrooms in K through 8 school settings throughout New England, New York, Puerto Rico, and the U.S. Virgin Islands. From these data, we have drawn the image of dynamic teachers and the roles they perform. To complete the picture, we integrated these data with examples from our previous work and years of experience in schools and with our knowledge of theory, research, and the work of other service providers and educational reformers.

Dynamic Teachers is not a case study of a select number of exemplary teachers teaching in innovative schools. We have seen teachers striving to enact the roles of dynamic teachers regardless of the realities of their individual school situations. Maggie and Don, and the school where they teach, are composite characters. We have intentionally used examples from a broad range of schools—some schools are among the most innovative and responsive to children, some are struggling to survive the turmoil that surrounds them. Although the examples focus largely on elementary and middle schools, our experience in high schools has shown us that dynamic teachers practice at all levels.

Finally, we have drawn heavily on our values about children and about learning. *Dynamic Teachers* is, therefore, research based, experience based, and values based.

Acknowledgments

We are grateful to many people for their help in creating this volume. Our colleagues at the Laboratory have been patient and understanding while our minds and hours have been occupied with this book; we thank them. Specifically, we acknowledge Janet Angelis for her editorial assistance, Dorys Popovich-Brennan for her word-processing assistance and general spirit lifting, Carol Godfrey and Mary Stenson for their work on the references, and Gretchen Anderson for editorial assistance. Last, but by far most important, we are extremely grateful to Glen Harvey, the acting executive director of the Laboratory; without her contributions to the original conceptualization of this project and her ongoing support, *Dynamic Teachers* would not have been possible.

We give special thanks to Bethany Rallis. She would involuntarily eavesdrop on meetings we held at her home; the comments she offered on our work always brought us back to the realities of the classroom and reminded us that, although dynamic teachers do exist, our schools need more.

Our appreciation also goes to all the schools and teachers and students who tolerated our presence and provided inspiration. Above all, we thank the many dynamic teachers who have served as models for the roles we explicate in this book. Seeing you in action ensures us that dynamic teachers *do* exist.

The work on which this publication is based is sponsored in part by the U.S. Department of Education, Office of Educational Research and Improvement, under contract to the Regional Laboratory for Educational Improvement of the Northeast and Islands (number RP-91-002-008). The contents of this publication do not necessarily reflect the views of the department or any other agency of the U.S. government.

About the Authors

Sharon F. Rallis is Program Coordinator of the Designing Schools for Enhanced Learning (DSEL) Initiative of the Regional Laboratory for Educational Improvement of the Northeast and Islands (the Regional Lab), a school transformation network of schools in the Northeast, Puerto Rico, and St. Croix. She came to the Lab from Peabody College of Vanderbilt University, where she was Associate Professor of Education in the Department of Educational Leadership. She has been a classroom teacher at all levels from K through 12, a counselor, a school principal, and an elected school board member. She was a senior research associate in a university center for evaluation and research, where she worked with teachers, principals, and superintendents, and helped develop and evaluate various educational programs at a state department of education. She is coauthor of *Principals of Dynamic Schools: Taking Charge of Change* (with Ellen B. Goldring) and *Becoming a School Board Member* (with Lee G. Bolman and Terrence E. Deal). She received her doctorate from Harvard University.

Gretchen B. Rossman is Professor of Education at the University of Massachusetts at Amherst, where she coordinates the Educational Administration Program. She also has served as the external evaluation consultant of the DSEL Initiative of the Regional Lab. She formerly served as Senior Research Associate and Director of Policy Studies at Research for Better Schools in Philadelphia. She has taught at the elementary school level and has served as a consultant for state departments of education, local school districts and schools, university research centers, and state and regional superintendent and principal associations. She is coauthor of *Change and Effectiveness in Schools: A Cultural Perspective* (with H. Dickson Corbett and William A. Firestone), *Designing Qualitative Research* (with Catherine Marshall), and *Mandating Academic Excellence: High School Responses to State Initiated Curriculum Reform* (with Bruce L. Wilson). She received her doctorate from the University of Pennsylvania.

Janet M. Phlegar is Deputy Director of the Regional Lab. She has been a classroom teacher at the elementary, middle, high school, and college levels in Atlanta, Detroit, and the Philippines. She also managed a division of a national educational foundation in Washington, D.C., and has consulted for state departments of education. She is currently the President of her community's local education foundation.

Ann Abeille is Internal Program Evaluator of the DSEL Initiative of the Regional Lab. Her previous evaluation work has focused on various reforms in urban school districts in the northeastern United States. She teaches evaluation in two Boston area colleges and has also taught at the middle and secondary school levels.

1

Dynamic Teachers

Introducing Their Challenges and Perspectives

Who are dynamic teachers? What makes them different from other teachers? What forces in schools today shape these teachers' behaviors? What demands and challenges do they face? Maggie and Don introduce roles they choose to perform as they seek to ensure that their students will thrive in today's complex world.

Maggie Clark climbed into her car and drove away from the O'Henry School. She was exhausted and the day had been long—but good. Before school, she had met with the Kiefers about Wanda's individualized education plan. Because Maggie team taught a multiage group, meeting Wanda's needs had been relatively easy—easier than dealing with Jonathan last week. Jonathan was noisy; he grunted and shouted while he worked. Maggie and her partner were working with the class to remind Jonathan to control his use of loud sounds, but they needed his parents to do the same at home. Jonathan's parents seemed overwhelmed with their own concerns for him. Maggie thought about how these children's special needs had grown into an important focus of her teaching—and how much she had come to enjoy these children in class.

The meeting with the Kiefers had been in a small space off the common area for Maggie's grouping, so she had not had to rush to be there when the children arrived. Maggie was pleased with the new building. She had served on the committee that had helped design the interior. She remembered long hours with the architect asking, What would a perfect learning space look like? How can we build that into a school? The result, the product of many compromises, included various spaces to accommodate different activities and alternative groupings. Today, she was especially glad to be there to greet the children as they brought in the first of their materials for setting up a frontier village in the common area. Rosita was struggling with something that resembled a mortar and pestle.

"Ah, Rosita, I remember; you're the baker. What do you have here?" asked Maggie.

"I will use it to grind corn. I was going to get ideas from the woman at Dough Boy. But my grandma told me about this. Kinda cool, isn't it?" smiled the little girl. "Farmers will bring me corn. Here, I'll show you how it works."

"Is that hard work? What would happen if farmers brought in a lot of corn all at once?" asked Maggie.

"I guess I'd get pretty tired of grinding. It's pretty fun to do just this much. Doing this all day would be boring, too. It takes a long time to do just a little. I don't think I'd have time to do any baking!" pondered Rosita.

"What might be some ways to do it easier?" Maggie and Rosita agreed that the villages must have had a more efficient way to grind large quantities of grain and that Rosita would explore the possibilities.

Maggie Clark had been teaching at O'Henry for 11 years. She had taught at several grade levels, but 2 years ago she and Don Medeiros decided to team up in teaching an age span of 3 years. Only one other multiage team existed in the school, although several other teams were sprinkled in schools throughout the district. Silvia O'Reilly and Judy Cohen had been team teaching in some form or other for what seemed like forever, and Maggie and Don often tested ideas out on them.

Don was an ideal partner—he and Maggie shared the same goals for children, and she often felt he was able to take their plans a step further than she could have alone. With the kids, they had generated the idea of setting up an authentic frontier village for their study of pioneers, but Don had pushed the idea of each member of the class "adopting" a local merchant to help construct and supply the different shops they would need. Don was always crossing the bridge between the classroom and the community. In fact, Don had been at a community school council meeting before school that morning.

Thinking about the community reminded Maggie of the debate about starting a two-way bilingual program in O'Henry. Recently Lee Palmer, the principal, had asked Don and Maggie to help sort out the various viewpoints: How many families would support it? Which plan would be best for O'Henry? Which teachers would be involved? "We need to find out what is best for our school. And we need to communicate with parents on this one."

Language differences had added a new twist to the challenge of communicating with parents. The community had changed a lot in the past decade. More and more children were coming to school with limited English skills. Maggie enjoyed the richness of a classroom buzzing with the sound of several languages, but at times she felt overwhelmed with the challenge of teaching children whose first language was not English. And she was bothered when she often had to wait for a translator to talk to a parent.

"Still, sometimes, when there is no language barrier, parents cannot help," Maggie thought. "Take Billy Nadler. He picked a fight—again—before PE class. He's always picking fights. Sure, his father is abusive and his home situation is rotten. But that's only an explanation. I won't accept it as an excuse. I will not allow him to fight. But what do we do? I feel helpless because we cannot suspend him or send him home. The 'island' has worked up until now—and having Sonia, the student teacher, in the class has helped. She can go sit by him when he goes to the island. Today someone got hurt—not bad— but anything at all is too much! Don and I—with a lot of help—have to keep on trying. We need to get beyond having an eye on him all the time. I get a little scared that someday when our eyes are not on him, he will really hurt someone. I honestly do not know what to do with him—and I'm mad too, because he really messes up my class."

The most frustrating part of the day, Maggie thought as she neared home, had been with a group of her colleagues. Nobody at the lunch table had agreed that new and more authentic assessment measures were essential. She had said she could not think of the last time she explained the "right way to do it" to the whole class, so why would she test her class on the "right way"? Why wasn't anyone else concerned about better ways to measure learning? Don was not at lunch, so she found herself alone and discouraged.

Maggie felt especially discouraged with Betty. Betty and Maggie had been friends since college, but Betty had become so narrow-minded and traditional. All Betty talked about was drawers full of "successful lessons." Maggie saw that for Betty, teaching was opening a drawer, pulling out a file, passing out the worksheets, and "watching the little ones learn." Maggie wanted to scream when Betty lectured about her freedom to teach the way she had been trained .

"Betty doesn't even think about her teaching. She just says, 'True/false tests work for me.' I ask her how she knows they work, and she says because she has been using them for years. Why won't she even consider that other ways may be possible? Or better?" wondered Maggie.

"Of course, the system doesn't help," lamented Maggie. "Parents are scared of new ideas for grading their kids, but we don't have any forums to share our thinking. It seems all the superintendent ever cares about is what people will think. 'Don't rock the boat' translates into 'Don't try anything new.' Even when some of us do coalesce on something like assessment, the district pulls out its support. Or the state issues a new mandate, and then we have to change direction."

In search of some control over her professional life, Maggie had become active in the teachers' association. Today had ended with an association board meeting. Maggie was reaching the end of her first term on this board. Today's discussion was about the increasing number of safety issues for teachers. Litigation, neighborhood violence, weapons in schools—all issues were raised to illustrate the need for new contract protections for teachers. Maggie had asked that additional professional development funds be used to prepare school professionals to deal with these problems better. She doubted that more restrictions on contracted hours or on interactions with kids or bigger insurance policies would make schools safer. The board had decide to hire a consultant to address school violence throughout the district.

The warm lights of home greeted Maggie as she turned into her driveway. On balance, the day had been good because of interactions with children like Rosita about grinding grain or the discovery she and Joel made about clocks and time in frontier towns. Then she remembered she had not returned a call to Mrs. Garman, Josie's mom. "I got too busy. It's easy to forget the Mrs. Garmans because Josie is a good student, and Mrs. Garman is not likely to make trouble. I really wish I had reached her today, but I can't do everything. So . . . I have tomorrow. . . ."

* * * * *

Who Are Dynamic Teachers?

Maggie—and her partner Don—represent a new kind of teacher in today's schools. What differentiates them from their colleagues is the way they know themselves, the way they look at children, their understanding of what it means to learn, and the way they interact with their students and the material they are teaching. They have chosen to teach because they believe that each child deserves multiple opportunities to construct and test his or her own meanings for the world about him or her. They see the purpose of their teaching as enhancing each child's chance for a full life. They bring their own genuine passion for learning to each child.

Maggie and Don recognize, but are not overwhelmed by, the challenges they face. Like others, they struggle with a changing world outside the school and a changing classroom inside. Much of what they do has been done by good teachers throughout the ages, but new and complex forces are at play in the world today—forces that affect schools and present those working in them with new demands. Being a good teacher now requires taking on new roles. The traditional role expected of teachers in the past—as a deliverer of information—will not suffice to meet the needs of students today.

Today, teachers find their interactions with children more complex as they inquire into questions the children raise and as they assess student progress in building answers for those questions. Their roles also extend beyond the classroom into the community. Maggie and Don do not allow the complexities of the classroom and community and their incumbent demands to discourage or paralyze them. Rather, they see the demands as resources or opportunities. They recognize and respond to the challenges by adopting new roles. They become facilitators, inquirers, bridgers, and changemakers. Teachers like Maggie and Don are what we call "dynamic teachers."

Dynamic teachers are able to assume these new roles because they bring so much to their teaching. They are moral stewards, constructors, and philosophers. They draw from a strong base of values, knowledge, skills, and professional commitment. Their clearly articulated value system is deeply grounded in the rights of children and families; their knowledge base is self-constructed yet connected to the culturally accepted knowledge of the field; they understand how people grow, develop, and learn; their skills are tried in experience; their professional practice is guided by a philosophy of reflection, action, and accountability. Daily, they visit and revisit their philosophy, checking to make sure their actions reflect their values.

But dynamic teachers are not successful in all the roles in which they find themselves. Many of these roles emerge as the teacher develops and understands the environment in different ways. Teachers play different roles more fully at different stages of their careers (Huberman, 1994). All teachers, however, make choices based on their own strengths, their experiences, and their particular settings. Not every dynamic teacher will take the lead, as Maggie and Don do; some will play supporting roles. Maggie, for example, has chosen to serve on the teachers' association board, whereas Don has recognized his skill and interest in bridging the school and community.

We will see the student teacher Sonia develop into a dynamic teacher as she adapts to several roles at the O'Henry School. She learns to make choices about the kind of teacher she wants to be to meet her students' varied needs.

These teachers are real. We have seen, talked to, worked with, and heard stories about these teachers as we have worked in schools that are choosing to transform. We have met Maggies and Dons in small schools and in large schools, in wealthy suburbs and in poor sections of cities. We have seen them at work in rural and in urban schools. Sometimes they are young and naive, and other times they are mature and experienced. They teach youngsters from every kind of home with every kind of background and need. Although we have placed Maggie and Don in an elementary school, we have seen dynamic teachers at work in high schools, though not as frequently. Although the roles remain the same, the challenges at the secondary level differ.

Often Maggie or Don are anomalies among their peers; sometimes, they work among like colleagues in a dynamic school (see Goldring & Rallis, 1993, Chap. 2); usually they work in a school with some who see the world as they do as well as with others who do not. In many respects Maggie and Don are lucky. They have each other, a few other supportive colleagues, and a school system that, for the most part, encourages their efforts. Not every teacher is so lucky. Some feel thoroughly isolated—a sole teacher striving for reform against a tide of complacency and mediocrity. Many feel resistance to change. Some feel supported—a member of a faculty that has embraced the challenge to value each and every child. Most find themselves somewhere in between, working with some like-minded colleagues within a larger, more reticent, often burned-out school faculty.

Community support varies as well. The community surrounding O'Henry includes folks who encourage the work of the professionals in their schools and who willingly participate in school activities. Yet Maggie and Don know that many parents and community members are disengaged from the work of the school, whereas others are skeptical of any perceived innovations. They can recall the struggle several years ago to pass the bond for the new school building. Those who had no school-age children put up a powerful opposition. Maggie and Don have learned they must work with the entire community to achieve the best education for all children.

Maggie and Don are not superteachers. They make mistakes. They get tired. They have limits, and, often they feel failure. Although occasionally they become overwhelmed, they always know why they are teaching. They see each child as a unique individual who can learn, and they understand the complexity and the responsibility of the task they have accepted. They know they cannot control all the forces affecting their classrooms, so they work with the forces. In this chapter, we introduce the forces with which dynamic teachers must contend as well as some strong barriers to change, and we describe how dynamic teachers view these forces and their worlds.

Forces Behind the Challenges in Today's Classroom

This new image of the dynamic teacher is of a professional who has assumed new roles in a positive response to the challenges in today's classroom. The roles these teachers play emerge from their recognition that the postmodern world is complex, paradoxical, and contested (see Hargreaves, 1994, Chap. 4, for a discussion of the changing contexts of education). Educators have always faced stubborn challenges. But today it is difficult to read a newspaper and not see that the realities of children's lives make the task of helping them think and learn formidable. New and complex forces, coming from both inside and outside the school, are placing totally different demands on teachers. Although many people can opt to disregard the realities these forces bring, teachers cannot. Children carry their lives with them into the classroom. By looking at some of the forces that influence the school, we can better understand Maggie's and Don's behavior and why dynamic teachers evolve.

Almost any aspect of society we might focus on reveals evidence of a change that can affect schools; most, such as globalization of information and communication, are common knowledge. We choose five major forces, some internal to the school and some external, that we believe directly affect teachers and contribute to the emergence of dynamic teachers:

- Student bodies today are more diverse with varied needs.
- Parents and community groups have more influence on the school.

- The social, economic, and technological needs of the workplace require new qualities and skills.
- Public demand for results has produced federal and state mandates and an overabundance of special programs.
- General acceptance of the status quo in education creates barriers to improvement.

Recognizing and acknowledging that these forces exist is the first step in addressing them. Teachers have several options in dealing with the forces: They can ignore them—to the peril of the classroom and children; they can react to them—and allow them to drive their curriculum and classroom; or they can take charge—using them to shape a dynamic classroom. The teacher who takes charge is one we call a dynamic teacher.

More Diverse Student Bodies

If we look into Maggie's and Don's classroom, we see an array of colors and languages and national heritages, as well as abilities and special needs. We see Wanda and Jonathan, who have identified disabilities; Rosita, whose family speaks Spanish at home; Billy, who every afternoon must return to an abusive home; Joel, whose intellect pushes beyond everyday understandings; and Lin Pao, who is new to the United States.

The differences in today's student body are deeper than physical. Each student comes with a variety of needs. Many are poor; others are emotionally or socially impoverished. Some know only a language other than English; others have specific learning disabilities. Some have medical needs, large or small. Many live with only one parent, and others are being raised by their grandparents. Several come to school hungry. The following statistics provide insight into the different life experiences of students today (Cooley, 1993):

- One of every two marriages ends in divorce.
- Twenty-four percent of all children under 18 live with one parent (nearly 70% of these children live with their mother).
- Fifty percent of women return to work before their child reaches 1.
- Nearly one of every six families with children was living in poverty in 1987.

- Nearly 16% of children are living in a stepfamily.
- The United States leads all developed countries in the number of teenagers giving birth and having abortions.
- Approximately 56 million American families indicate alcohol-related problems; 41% of families report child abuse.

The changing demographics of our nation today are reflected in every classroom. These children are in our schools—all our schools—and, to some extent, society looks to the schools to meet their needs. Along with special needs, diversity also brings new resources. Sometimes the resource is obvious; more often, it is not immediately apparent. The task of uncovering hidden talents, strengths, or knowledge falls to the teacher.

In sum, awareness of the needs, rights, and contributions of all of society's members places a vast set of demands and expectations on curricular, as well as extracurricular, offerings and on those who lead the school. This multicultural cornucopia can provide a rich resource if teachers can recognize and tap into it. Doing so, however, is a challenge. Today's teachers must expand their roles to deal with these issues.

Influence of Parents and Community Groups

Teachers are being called upon to be more responsive to the whole child. To do so, they must deal more directly than ever before with parents, parent groups, and community agencies. We see Maggie and Don meeting with parents for a variety of reasons. They know from the research that parental participation is an important component of the "effective school" (Clark, Lotto, & McCarthy, 1980). Whereas the research findings are mixed and seem to vary according to the social status of the parents, increased parent-school relationships appear to lead to significant educational benefits (Becker & Epstein, 1982; Hoover-Dempsey, Bassler, & Brissie, 1987). Thus Maggie and Don seek parent support whenever possible.

Dynamic teachers also recognize that, both in theory and in practice, schools are interconnected with their environments. Because they see the boundaries of educational organizations as permeable, boundary-spanning tasks become crucial. Events and attitudes in the community affect the school and their classroom, so Maggie and

Don have learned to know the community. They also find themselves seeking assistance and support from social service agencies that have previously been separate from the school.

"The school does not exist in a void" (Cunningham, 1990, p. 12). It is embedded in the social context of its surrounding communities. This social context has a tremendous effect on the classroom. Families with diverse structures, employment arrangements, and racial and ethnic backgrounds require new support systems. The school, as potentially the only stable institution in a community, plays a pivotal role in meeting this wider array of community needs. Schools can no longer close their doors to their surrounding communities.

A good example of the new demands being placed on schools as they are expected to help with the "total" needs of children are the integrated social services, also called "wrap-around services," connected to many schools. In many communities, schools and other social service agencies have joined together to coordinate a wide range of services for children and their families. The assistance provided includes medical services, general equivalency diploma (GED) preparation, employment counseling, housing assistance, and after-school care. Other integrated service programs focus on the health and nutritional needs of families, as well as linkages with community agencies (Crowson & Boyd, 1992).

These new initiatives, aimed at meeting the needs of a wide range of children and their families, place new and different demands on the school and its teachers. The school is no longer responsible only for educating the child; it is responsible for the total well-being of the child. Teachers now often must make decisions about programs and activities beyond the school curriculum. They interact with professionals outside the walls of the school. Teachers work with parents in a variety of capacities, not only as the parents of the students they teach in school.

Finally, dynamic teachers find themselves responding to parents who are members of groups working with the school. Much of the recent state reform legislation mandates that schools have local councils that include a minimum number of parent representatives. Although many of these councils are advisory and symbolic, others, such as the Chicago school councils, have authority to make policy, personnel, and budget decisions. Parents are also often active on special interest advocacy groups, such as the local advisory councils for special education, Chapter I, or bilingual education. Rather than resisting involvement with such groups, dynamic teachers like Maggie and Don have learned to use these avenues for interaction with parents to their benefit.

New Qualities and Skills Required

Postmodern economies offer more flexible work roles and labor processes than the standardization and mass production of the past. Connections between producer and consumer increase as technology becomes more sophisticated. Globalization changes the meaning of coordination and connection as ideas and products flow across national boundaries. The resulting new occupational and social structures call for new qualities and skills for the future workforce (Reich, 1992). Yesterday's effective school no longer suffices as a place to procure those qualities and skills. Because the details of tomorrow are uncertain, the definition of what must be known is emergent.

> Communication and technology are compressing space and time, leading to an increasing pace of change in the world we seek to know and in our ways of knowing it. This, in turn, threatens the stability and endurance of our knowledge bases, making them irretrievably fragile and provisional. (Hargreaves, 1994, p. 57)

As a result, teachers' work is intensified, "with teachers expected to respond to greater pressures and to comply with multiple innovations under conditions that are at best stable and at worst deteriorating" (Hargreaves, 1994, p. 118). Creating a classroom that can teach students how to get along in this new world as well as the skills to access and use available information and resources requires new pedagogy.

Amid this accelerated pace of change, schools cling to old and conventional operations. Thus teachers live with paradox. For example, technological advances and the information highway present a mixed blessing. Although the information available at the touch of a finger has increased exponentially, the demand to know more and use knowledge better has also increased. Yet a teacher's day remains locked in a traditional structure, with little time for communication and little or no access to computers or phone lines. Dynamic teachers are challenged to meet new expectations within old structures, as they work to change the structures.

Overabundance of Special Programs and State Mandates

Educators and parents, as well as legislators, are aware of schools' shortcomings. Everyone demands results, but no one agrees on what these results should be. Furthermore, generally accepted measures do not exist to determine what results are achieved. "Fixing" schools has meant applying bandages, with a resulting overloading of curriculum. Maggie and Don face conflicting messages from the public and policymakers: site-based management versus national standards, professionalism versus increased layperson control, an overabundance of special programs versus integrated curriculum.

Much state reform legislation has supported decentralization to bring the locus of decision making closer to the point of contact between student and teacher. Yet as Murphy (1991) notes,

> Freedom from district-level controls and restrictions imposed by union contracts will lead only to marginal increases in local options if state and federal government agencies continue to ensnarl schools in ever-expanding webs of regulations and prescriptions. (p. 42)

In the 1980s, numerous education reports (e.g., National Commission on Excellence in Education, 1983) alerted the public to what has become known as the crisis in schooling. Studies and reports continue to decry the decline in student outcome measures and American competitiveness in the world market. Recent efforts to establish national standards in various content areas are only one example of governmental response to public demand for improved results. The federal government, in supporting these efforts, has also directed some school improvement dollars through the states' departments of education to support local development of curriculum frameworks to match nationally defined standards.

This struggle between local, state, and national efforts also plays out in the profession's attempt to define itself. The federal and state push to establish goals and standards exists amid efforts already underway by various professional associations. The National Council of Teachers of Mathematics (NCTM, 1991), for example, is credited with developing the first national standards for what should be taught in a particular subject and how to teach it. Many professionals and policymakers, however, remain skeptical that all this activity around standards will result in any real improvement in student achievement (e.g., Goodman, 1994). Similarly, efforts such as those of the Northeast Common Market Project (a collaboration of the Regional Laboratory for Educational Improvement of the Northeast and Islands and several state departments of education) to create common professional certification standards that would apply throughout the region have come up against current state statutes.

At the same time, the professional educators and laypersons on local school councils disagree on decisions about school operations. Examples of compromises that benefit the children are few but do exist. In one such example, the teachers in an impoverished community submitted to the parents' wish to provide uniforms for students; they respected the parents' reasoning that uniforms would promote equity. On the other hand, the teachers insisted that classrooms be furnished with tables and work areas rather than the individual desks the parents chose. They felt that one decision called for professional expertise whereas the other had not.

Another result of public demand for services from schools has been the implementation of an overabundance of special programs. Programs targeted at every identifiable need fill the school curriculum. We have heard today's curriculum described as analogous to a cargo plane so overloaded that it cannot get off the ground.[1] Chapter I, remediation, resource assistance, bilingual and ESL students—whether pull-out or included—all affect classroom functioning. Specific requirements in health education, science education, language, physical education, arts education, and others fragment an already overloaded instructional program. We even know of one school committee that required several weeks of humane education for all third graders! In some schools, the number of programs has multiplied to the point that it is difficult to define what is part of one program and what is separate from it. In such cases, the availability of options can actually serve as a boon to the teacher who knows how to build an integrated curriculum.

Still, the burden to integrate falls on the teacher, and the disparity and number of programs can easily overwhelm the most innovative of teachers. This becomes an even greater problem when children are constantly pulled out of their home classroom. We have heard teachers express extreme frustration because they have their entire class together for as little as 20% of instructional time. They also describe children who remain confused most of the school day because they do not stay in one place, with one group, one teacher, or one focus for more than half an hour at a time.

Barriers to Improvement

The above forces have shaped a world that we accept as radically different from yesterday's. Yet schools have ignored these changes and resisted reformation. Schools are caught in an old paradigm, weighted down by their status quo. Because the public considers itself an insider in the field of education, unlike in business and industry, school leaders are constrained by an existing definition of what is schooling: "It is what *I* experienced" (see Meyer & Rowan, 1977). This counterforce of maintaining the status quo is the final force with which teachers must contend.

Rather than serving as a commonality from which schools may be reshaped, the public's previous experience in schools creates a barrier to change. In almost any school today one can feel the oppressive weight of "the way education has always been" inhibiting people from drastically rethinking the way education should be. Educators and parents alike are especially slow to change their tendencies to sort children, to limit learning to textbooks, and to cling to traditional time structures.

The old paradigm holds fast to the insidious practice of sorting children according to perceived abilities. Many parents who experienced this sorting and labeling as children expect and want to see the same arrangement for their own children, always with the hope that their child will come out on top of the pile, heading for college, a good job, and "success." Teachers consider the ability to make these judgments and sortings an essential part of the expertise they bring to the classroom. The language of this process of educators' deciding the fate of children is deeply embedded in the everyday

conversations of teachers with each other, with parents, and, perhaps most dangerously, with children.

Another part of the way things have always been in schools is
the degree to which education is bound, focused on, and limited to
the contents of textbooks. Teachers and parents alike experienced
school as a place where social studies, for example, was simply a
boring book made up mainly of term definitions and a few maps.
Ask most fourth graders today and they will respond that social
studies is a book with questions at the end of the chapters. And what
are parents and teachers seeking as reassurance that their children
are learning social studies? Many expect little more than memoriz-
ing definitions and answering the questions at the end of a chapter.
The omnipresence of these pabulum textbooks is a constant pressure
on teachers that children need them, that teachers have to use them,
and that as long as they use them, the children will learn "enough."

The third part of the status quo of education that has so far
written the rules of school is the established time structure—one that
was designed for children who have the luxury of one stay-at-home
parent and for teachers who expect to be tied to the school for only
6 hours a day 9 months a year. This rarely questioned schedule allows
teachers to do their correcting and planning at home while meeting
their own family and other commitments. This arrangement not
only limits student time on tasks and access to richer experiences
but also severely limits time for teachers to meet and plan together
so as to improve their work with children. Professional development
pursuits then must come out of class time with children and are
frequently viewed as separate, additional time commitments as
opposed to opportunities for growth provided as part of the job.

Dynamic teachers are able to reach beyond these traditional
meanings and structures of schools. Teachers like Maggie and Don
are responding to the forces acting on schools today to transform
their classrooms into places where all children can learn. They deal
with forces and overcome the barriers because they define learning
and the successful learner differently. They are moving beyond the
rhetoric to seek understandings to the following questions:

- What do we mean by learn?
- What do we mean by all children?
- How can they belong in our school?
- How can they experience success in our school?

Making a Difference for Children

Foundations for Learning

Dynamic teachers draw their understanding of learning from the progressive and pragmatic theories of knowledge of Pierce, James, and Dewey.[2] They posit that the human mind enables us to use experience to adapt for survival; thus meaning, truth, and knowledge are tightly tied to experience. When people learn, they construct their own meaning for an experience through their interaction with the event, object, person, idea, or activity. They question; they try out possible answers; they seek to fit the new information and understandings into their existing mental frameworks. Because each person brings a different set of prior experiences to each new experience, each person's construction or interpretation of the experience will be somewhat different.

But this construction is useful only when communicated and tested among others and within an existing culturally accepted body of knowledge (Cobb, 1994; Driver, Asoko, Leach, Mortimer, & Scott, 1994). Dewey notes that "the same existential events are capable of an infinite number of meanings" (quoted in Garrison, 1994, p. 11), and therefore, meanings are negotiated and validated through cooperative behavior. Knowledge, then, is a set of beliefs, socially constructed and communicated, that individuals use to navigate their everyday worlds. These interactions, or processes of inquiry, constitute learning, and learning requires both discovery and enculturation.

Learners need not only to act but also to know the meaning of their actions; not only to think but to understand the effect of their thinking. Classrooms like Maggie's and Don's enable students to act and to develop the skills to reflect on their actions. Students in these classrooms consciously construct meanings and negotiate the effect of their constructions. Maggie and Don encourage their students to test the validity of their constructions—to share the meanings they have developed with others so that they too can understand. Their goal is to develop shared constructs, with the ultimate goal of improving the everyday lives of individuals and society as a whole.

Recent research on brain development and work in cognitive psychology has established and confirmed that multiple complex and concrete experiences are essential for meaningful learning and teaching, and that the overwhelming need of learners is meaningfulness (e.g., Caine & Caine, 1991; Presidential Task Force on Psychology in Education, 1993). Creating such a rich, interactive, and complex environment filled with a mix of children with a range of backgrounds and abilities is more than advantageous; it is essential for learning.

Views of Children

Dynamic teachers see individual children, not categories. Although they believe all children learn, they know that each child uses a different approach and brings a somewhat different perspective. All children do not look alike, nor do they all think alike. Dynamic teachers create a classroom where *all* children belong—the athletic girl, the gifted boy, the class clown, the recent immigrant, the child whose parents do not speak English, the quiet one, the middle-of-the-road student.

Dynamic teachers do not ask *if* a student can learn or how much of a prescribed set of standards a student has achieved, but under what conditions a student *will* learn and to what knowledge, skills, and opportunities the student has access. The practice of these teachers is focused on the construction and use of knowledge by the students themselves. They judge success by the experiences they provide for the learner, on the meanings the learner creates out of the experiences, and on the ability of the learner to communicate and act on what he or she has learned. This means, by definition, that poor children, delinquent children, children with disabilities—all children—can and do make sense of their worlds; and they all need rich school environments and multiple opportunities to develop shared constructs that work in their worlds.

Dynamic teachers' classrooms are places where each child learns because the teachers recognize the value of children, diversity, and learning. Dynamic teachers believe that learning is natural, that diversity is a resource, that each child can contribute to an emerging society. Dynamic teachers see the purpose of schooling as enabling each child to reach his or her full potential within that emergent society. Their practice represents a radical shift from common practice—because many teachers still act to train and sort children to fit existing slots in a static workforce. The traditional classroom was not designed to make all children—disabled, minority, or "normal"—feel welcome, comfortable, and included.

The approach of a dynamic teacher, although alternative to that held by the traditional teacher, is not a new one. It has its roots in ancient Greece. A century ago, Rousseau wrote, "Each individual is born with a distinctive temperament." Yet Rousseau also recognized the prevailing tendency of schooling to ignore individuality:

> We indiscriminately employ children of different bents on the same exercises; their education destroys the special bent and leaves dull uniformity. Therefore after we have wasted our efforts in stunting the true gifts of nature we see the short-lived and illusory brilliance we have substituted die away, while the natural abilities we have crushed do not revive. (quoted in Dewey, 1966, p. 116)

The Maggies and Dons we have seen seek to nurture children's "special bents" and "natural abilities." When they look back at their own experiences of schooling, they question the practices and environments that smothered these qualities in children. They see that each person learns in a unique way, making his or her own sense of the world around him or her. In short, because dynamic teachers accept and value individual differences in learning, they believe that all people can learn.

The work of dynamic teachers is founded in a deep valuing of children as individuals and of children's learning. Childhood is not merely a step toward adulthood. Rather, childhood is a time to create and experiment—a time for each child to discover his or her world as well as his or her place in it. Maggie and Don see that the world tomorrow may be quite different from today's world. They see that today's knowledge and skills alone will not prepare children for tomorrow. They recognize that in tomorrow's workplace people will need to know how to frame problems to be solved. People will need confidence in their own abilities to access, organize, and use information and resources, rather than storing disconnected information in their brains. Thus the teaching of dynamic teachers goes beyond transmittal of the known; their teaching develops the natural ability to inquire—to frame essential questions and to seek meaningful ways to inform those questions in the child's life. In short, Maggie and Don respect and value the child's role in his or her own learning.

Practicing in a
Dynamic Classroom

Dynamic teachers practice what they teach. They reflect and inquire themselves. They ask, "If I value children and their role in their own learning, how do I design my classroom and my lessons? How do I know what students are learning? How can I be sure they are learning to their fullest potential and that their learning is useful to them?" Reflecting about their work—what succeeded, what did not, and what they could have done better—is a part of the lives of teachers like Maggie and Don. As constructivist learners, they must make their own sense of information and events. Constructing one's own meaning requires reflection and inquiry. Dynamic teachers are seldom satisfied simply to do something. They must analyze, synthesize, and evaluate it as well.

Maggie and Don—and Sonia, their student teacher—accept that they are learners themselves. They know they are constantly constructing their own meaning for the information they encounter and the activities they engage in. Their knowledge is a product of these constructions. To bring this knowledge to their students, they must persistently reexamine their understandings and be able to communicate them in clear and appropriate ways. As Maggie asked Rosita about grinding corn, she was building her own way of thinking about the process, even as she helped Rosita think about it and learn.

Action is equally important (see Fullan, 1993). Reflection is always connected to action. Dynamic teachers operate on a philosophy of professional commitment, with a base of values and guiding principles and the interacting elements of reflection and inquiry, initiative and action, and responsibility and accountability. This philosophy provides, paradoxically, both the safety and the freedom to take risks. Dynamic teachers feel comfortable taking novel or unusual actions because each action is based on an articulated value and is chosen after deep and thorough inquiry. They "construct" their risks.

The freedom to take risks comes from understanding themselves and the reasons behind their actions. Control is not an issue for dynamic teachers. They understand the paradox that to give up the effort to control students is to gain freedom and authority. They direct their efforts toward creating a safe environment in which students may make appropriate choices. For example, Maggie and Don designed their room so that children can do things for themselves—whether it be storing materials in low shelves, using child-sized furniture, or creating rich work spaces. Thus their time is not spent getting or finding things for the children or telling children what and how to act. They have freed themselves to interact more directly with the children's thinking about what they are doing. Although many traditional teachers arrange their rooms similarly, what dynamic teachers do differently is to ensure that they vest responsibility for the use of space and behavior within that space with the children.

Finally, dynamic teachers are accountable for their actions. They seek evidence of the connection between an action and the driving values and the action's effect. They ask, "What is the outcome? How do the outcomes relate to my purposes and goals? Are these socially and morally acceptable outcomes? Do students, parents, and community members understand the outcomes? How are the outcomes received?" They take responsibility for their work. Ensuring that their classroom provides an environment where all children can learn means that they must extend their influence beyond the classroom. They interact with their colleagues, parents, and the community; with members of the educational hierarchy; and, if necessary, with policymakers. They do not wait for the conditions of teaching to change; they help make the changes happen.

SUMMARY

Dynamic teachers recognize and respond to the forces that have shaped richer but more complex and challenging classrooms than ever before. In their work, they integrate their beliefs about children, about learning, and about knowledge and its construction into the roles they assume. Dynamic teachers know themselves and what they value. They frame and inform questions about what kind of classroom they want. They take thoughtful action and they consider the effects of their actions. Having accepted accountability to the children they serve, they work to improve their practice. This guiding philosophy of professional commitment is an essential part of every dynamic teacher's practice and of every role a dynamic teacher plays. Dynamic teachers are moral stewards, constructors, and philosophers.

These teachers choose new roles—the facilitator, the inquirer, the bridger, the changemaker—to create an environment where all children can make sense of their world in ways that will enable them to contribute positively to an emerging society. As we will illustrate throughout the following chapters, dynamic teachers' commitment to children is not rhetorical; rather, it is very real—and extremely difficult to achieve in a culture that pays lip service to the well-being and primacy of its children. In the next few chapters, we explore the values, the knowledge, and the skills dynamic teachers have.

Notes

1. We cannot remember exactly where we heard this analogy, but we think Fenwick English used it in a speech to a state's annual meeting of the Association for Supervision and Curriculum Development sometime in the last few years.

2. This discussion of pragmatism and progressivism is drawn from the following works: Dewey (1966), Garrison (1994), James (1918), and Soltis (1994).

The Moral Steward

Honoring Human Rights and Responsibilities

Dynamic teachers hold a set of values that drives their actions. Certain values specifically affect their relationships with children. What do we mean by values? What values do these teachers hold? How do these values shape the learning environment? How do dynamic teachers act on their values? Maggie and Don demonstrate their values in their classroom.

"You never seem to give up on Frannie. I don't see how you do it! Whenever I'm working with her, I find I have to go through each step with her—even then she seldom gets it. Today, I saw you helping her cut a piece of paper and then fit the pieces together. She still didn't seem to see the point. Why do you keep trying?" Sonia asked Maggie over a cup of tea at the end of the day. Sonia had been with Maggie and Don for more than a month now.

"Well, maybe it's because I know she'll get it. We just haven't found the right connections for her. Don't you think Frannie can make sense of parts and a whole—as can any other kid?" Maggie responded.

"Well, sure, but why give her more chances than any other kid?"

" I guess I don't look at it that way—I don't see that I'm giving her more chances. She's learning. We just haven't found

the right conditions for her yet. Did you notice how she began
to put those blocks together after she sat with Amid and Karin
this afternoon?" Maggie asked.

"I did. It was like something hit her. All of a sudden she
was doing it! Are you saying that maybe she needed to see other
children do it first?" wondered Sonia.

"Something like that. Can't be sure what. Possibly, she
needed all the different stimuli—and finally it clicked for her."

"Do you really, honestly believe that everyone can learn
at high levels?" pushed Sonia.

"Sure I do. Everyone's mind and experiences are so different that we cannot expect people to all get it the same way.
That's the problem with so much of school—kids have to fit one
mold. That isn't good for kids. And our world loses as well.
We need all the different ideas and mindsets. How would we
ever discover new ways to do things? Take Einstein as a student. Considered a failure in school. But under different conditions, he was a genius," Maggie observed.

"So maybe Frannie is a genius in disguise?"

"Maybe. Maybe not. But you think Roger is a genius,
don't you?" laughed Maggie.

"Aw, he's just a lively boy who doesn't want to sit still. I
know he's smart when he is interested in something," protested
Sonia.

"See! There you have it! Find the right conditions," concluded Maggie.

"I know you're right, but you seem so sure of yourself
about reaching all kids. How did you get that way?"

"I do a lot of thinking about what's important to me . . .
about what I value in teaching. I had a kid brother who was
in a lot of trouble. He dropped out of school when he turned
16. Teachers always said he was a stupid troublemaker. They
didn't appreciate that he'd wire their desks so that the Rolling
Stones would play when a drawer was opened. After he
dropped out, he got a job building televisions . . . until they
discovered he didn't have a diploma. He's never been able to
hold a job—yet I think he is a genius. I often think how he might

have led a different life if some teacher had taken the time to see that he was good and bright behind all his different-ness," mused Maggie.

"So . . . you see your brother in a lot of kids?" suggested Sonia.

"I'd say I see a lot of kids who are worth a lot—none are worth writing off the way Paul was."

"But don't the students have some responsibility? The teacher can't do it all!" said Sonia.

"Absolutely. The student is the worker. We don't work for them. But this is where our high expectations come in."

"You mean we have to let them know they can do it," Sonia agreed.

"And that they have to do it themselves! I once had a student who was a real prankster—a master at playing tricks on his classmates and us. Lively kid. I really liked him. He came back to visit after he moved beyond our class. We became close. Kevin wanted to become a firefighter. Whenever he'd hear the fire whistle he'd jump on his bike and follow the trucks. On one adventure, a car hit him. Spinal damage. Became a paraplegic in a wheelchair. I'd visit him often . . . in the hospital, when he came home. I wanted to help him, but the visits became a burden to me because he kept waiting for me to make something good happen. One day I got angry with him—told him *he* had to do it—whatever it was he wanted. I told him I wasn't going to visit again until he did something."

"So . . . what happened?" asked Sonia.

"It took a while, but he did things all right. That was back before there was a movement advocating rights for people with disabilities. Kevin was in on the ground floor of that movement. He got wheelchair ramps cut into the sidewalks at corners so he could get himself around town, for example. Of course, he wouldn't talk to me for a long time! He still thinks I was unfair," Maggie smiled, remembering.

"Kevin's story helps me. Your values are so clear it's almost as though they have faces on them," Sonia said with admiration.

*   *   *   *   *

Maggie's values are clear to herself and to others. The clarity of her values is one of the characteristics that makes her a dynamic teacher. Another defining characteristic is her willingness to accept responsibility for her actions and to require her students to do the same. In other words, she acts with purpose, and she considers the effect of her actions. She expects the same of her students and clearly articulates this expectation. Maggie and Don consider each human worthwhile and deserving of a full life. Their teaching is driven by their belief that the purpose of education is to ensure that each person reaches his or her potential for a full life. They value people and their potential. What do we mean by values and how do these play out in the work of dynamic teachers?

Values of Dynamic Teachers

Foundation for Action

Values are beliefs that drive action. All people possess values by which they live. These values may be conscious or unconscious; they may be articulated or not. The term *values* tends to be overused—in politics, the media, and everyday conversation. Today, the word implies self-righteousness and that the values the speaker espouses, for example, family values, are self-evident and necessarily good. We neither imply nor assume righteousness. Rather, we emphasize that people hold a complex set of values, some that express moral principles and others that are hurtful. Most important, people very often do not understand or have never explored which values lie behind their own or others' actions. Argyris and Schon (1978), for example, describe inconsistencies between what people say— their espoused theory—and what we can actually see them do—their theory-in-use. People act on their deeply held values—and these may not be the ones they have articulated!

The value-driven actions of teachers affect the lives and futures of children. Therefore, teachers' value bases need to be explicated. Teachers, like other people, have conscious and unconscious values about all aspects of their lives. Our focus is directed toward those values and assumptions that relate to schoolchildren, their families, and the responsibilities of teachers (Astuto, Clark, Read, McGree, & Pelton Fernandez, 1993). Dynamic teachers consciously hold a defined set of values about children, teaching, and learning. Their teaching reflects these values. Maggie's and Don's actions illustrate the values of dynamic teachers.

Human Rights for Children

Simply put, the values of dynamic teachers center around a strong belief in the basic human rights of children and their families. Our understanding of human rights consists of the social, cultural, political, and civic rights identified and promoted by the Universal Declaration of Human Rights adopted and proclaimed by the United Nations General Assembly on December 10, 1948 (see Appendix B). These articulated rights recognize knowledge about other people, foster attitudes of tolerance and respect, and promote awareness of individual responsibilities to treat all people with dignity (Torney-Purta, 1984). Human rights promote prosocial behavior, that is, "behavior that benefits other people" (Staub, 1979, p. 2).

Specific values vary among the many individuals whom we would call dynamic teachers, but all dynamic teachers share a common sense of the worth of the human being. They also possess the ability to understand a situation from another person's point of view (Kohlberg, 1969). Although our intent is not to delineate all human rights, we will review the fundamentals of a human rights value system that apply to learning because, in school settings, the rights of children and their families cannot be forgotten or dismissed.

Dynamic teachers believe in the educability of all students (Purpel, 1989); thus, they believe that every child they teach has the right to favorable conditions (time, quality of instruction, content, opportunity to interact with appropriate materials) for learning (Murphy & Hallinger, 1984). Dynamic teachers' values include respect for individual differences and for an individual's right to a voice within the classroom. These teachers see that honoring "the dignity of each person" and seeking to ensure "that each person enjoy(s) a fully human life" (Starratt, 1991, p. 195) are legitimate educational goals.

Recognizing the inherent value of all persons frees teachers to encourage students to work together to develop undiscovered outcomes. Although teachers value existing knowledge, they equally value knowledge building. Thus, they value a child's capacity to construct knowledge (Bransford, 1991; Cohen, 1988) and see their classrooms as places to build children's capabilities and to encourage them "to develop ways and means for using their capabilities" (Sergiovanni, 1989, p. 39). They value students as workers (Sizer, 1984), and believe that all students can reason critically and use higher order thinking skills (Howard, 1991).

Although they encourage children to use these skills and to work together, dynamic teachers do not minimize the difficult challenges they encounter in children who are outcasts in the classroom, those who resist engagement in classroom activities, and those who try to control the attention and time of the teacher and other children through disruptive behavior. The teacher's role is to help children discover their own value and that of others as learners in and positive contributors to the classroom community. The teacher's role is also to facilitate this process—creating a learning environment in which students can taste knowledge, discover and dig deeply into a broad expanse of content areas, test their own understandings, and share with others to build greater understandings. The teacher's responsibility is to ensure that each child is reaping the maximum benefits from this process and environment. (See Fullan, 1993, Chap. 2, for a discussion of managing moral purpose in the classroom.)

Dynamic teachers are guided by ethics of caring, collaboration, and empowerment rather than ethics of competition, utility, and control (Astuto et al., 1993; Beck, 1991). Valuing diversity complements and extends valuing commonality; one important aspect of diversity is each individual's contribution to the community. Dynamic teachers see education as human development unfolding within social communities of learning (Barth, 1986; Bransford, 1991). Thus, dynamic teachers encourage children to work and learn together.

Action and critical reflection are essential elements of a dynamic teacher's value system. Acting on their beliefs and accepting responsibility for the effect of their actions are themselves important values for these teachers. For them, vision emerges from action more than it precedes action, especially because dynamic teachers seek shared vision that can evolve only through dynamic interaction with others (Fullan, 1993). The learning that grows out of the inquiry associated with action is a valued part of the process.

Values for a Learning Environment

Establishing New Balance

Maggie and Don put the rights of children in the forefront of their work through ongoing inquiry into their practice. They clearly accept responsibility for the effect of their personal interactions with children and families, as well as for the learning environment they provide for children. They know their job is to ensure that the essential human rights of children are not lost—in either the pursuit of curriculum coverage or the maintenance of power, tradition, or structures. They recognize that these essential rights belong to *all* of their students and that with these rights come obligations and responsibilities for children. Dynamic teachers have seen that unless the rights operate in conjunction with corollary responsibilities, the learning environment can break down. Children can disengage from the community or channel their energy into draining power struggles.

Maggie's and Don's values drive them to create learning environments that balance the need for rights and responsibilities— learning communities in which each individual treats others and is treated with respect. Dynamic teachers believe that this balance is essential for building positive self-concept in children and for every child to feel that he or she is safe and belongs. In this safe environment where they feel valued, children contribute to their own learning; they are able to understand the relevance of learning to their lives and to become self-reliant in the pursuit of learning.

Children in classes like Maggie's and Don's become part of a learning community. Such a community recognizes and helps in the discovery and appreciation of the multiple talents and strengths of each child and encourages action. Students take ownership of their learning and behavior and become significant contributors to their collaborative learning community. They stand up for their own rights and also work for the rights of others who may, for whatever reason, be oppressed. They enter into a covenant, that is, an agreement that honors both their individuality and the community they are building. (This important concept is discussed more fully in Chapter 7.) The children establish balances between the following:

- the challenge of individual achievement and the richness of learning with and from others through collaboration, in which they discover and build on each others' strengths;
- working under the guidance of a wise and knowledgeable teacher and developing trust in their own abilities and thinking; and
- behaving "under control" because they respect others and exploring together actively, enthusiastically, and in a communicative manner.

To create such rich learning environments, Maggie and Don reach deep inside of themselves, exploring their innermost beliefs, fears, reactions, and assumptions about people different from themselves—whether in race, culture, language, religion, physical ability, gender, economic status, or general life situation. In addition, they examine their own learning styles and explore ways to build on the multiple learning styles, intelligences, and interests of the children in their classrooms. These are teachers who are not afraid of professional self-examination, which can also become very personal.

Dynamic teachers pose as a stark contrast to colleagues who blame families, neighborhoods, cultures, or other external circumstances for the struggles in their schools and classrooms. The more traditional teacher seeks external responsibility for children who are outcasts in their classrooms, unengaged in the learning, and falling hopelessly behind. Blaming others is easy when students fail, when they refuse to enter into classroom activities, or when they use misbehavior to control the environment.

Dynamic teachers choose not to blame others. This does not mean that they ignore failure or wallow in guilt. Rather, they consider all possible causes for failures or misbehavior. They do not have magic answers. They do not seek outside excuses. They ask the hard questions: What does this child need? How can I adjust the environment so these children can succeed? With the children themselves, dynamic teachers seek answers. Teachers like Maggie and Don accept the difficulties and know that their job is to help children find their own answers, strategies, and sense of self-respect.

When teachers take on the responsibility for children's human rights in schools, they adopt a paradigm of education that places the learner at the center. They reject the old factory-based paradigm that views children as raw material with predetermined worth, only the most deserving of whom will survive (Astuto et al., 1993). From the new perspective, teachers see each learner as deserving a chance.

These teachers' values extend beyond intellectual musings about educating perfect children from perfect families in perfect settings. The values of dynamic teachers are, above all, reality based—based on who their students really are, not who the teachers might wish they were. The teachers recognize and work with the specific talents, experiences, and interests that the students bring, not necessarily the ones with which the teachers may feel most comfortable.

Although dynamic teachers hold a vision of what they hope to accomplish over a school year, they demonstrate extraordinary suppleness in adapting that vision to best meet the needs of the actual students. Dynamic teachers use their professional knowledge and experience to choose these adaptations. They recognize that children change, grow, and develop—from day to day and year to year. Dynamic teachers actively look for behaviors that reveal these changes. They do not expect to create the same learning environment each day or each year.

For example, two dynamic teachers who work together in a multiage classroom in a small rural school report their regret at having to increase the degree of structure in the classroom one year; the change ran counter to their vision of the ideal classroom, but they recognized that this particular group of children worked better with more direction and a clear structure. Therefore, they imposed more direction and structure that year.

Another dynamic teacher reveals her deep consciousness of her values in the following excerpt from her professional portfolio: "The classroom should

- allow time and space for each child's voice;
- immerse children in content, i.e., literature, real math problems, writing for real purposes;
- allow children to interact directly with the materials and concepts;
- focus on the children's, not the teacher's or curriculum's, needs; and
- use what children bring with them from outside the school setting."[1]

When teachers are able to change their thinking and practice to make the environment fit their students and students' talents, rather than the reverse, they achieve new and richer learning environments.

Connecting With Families

Maggie and Don know that creating a balanced environment requires that they develop a deep understanding of the individual children they teach. This understanding includes an awareness of the lives of the children outside school. The children's family lives are often unlike their own. Their customs and expectations may differ (Criscoe, 1995). They may come from a different culture. A child may live with two parents or one, or with uncles, aunts, grandparents, older siblings, or other guardians. Family members may speak languages other than English; they may not know how to read.

Dynamic teachers know that sometimes families are willing and able to help; sometimes, however, they are not or cannot. The family may be overwhelmed with the struggles of unemployment, or parents' jobs may not allow them to attend school functions. The family may have to struggle to feed, clothe, or shelter children. The family may face a devastating illness or loss. Adults' own negative memories of schools and teachers may stand in the way of their involvement with the children's school. For Maggie and Don, their own responsibility as teachers cannot be any less, no matter what the family situation might be.

Some children may feel that the school rejects their background and family. An adversarial relationship between school or teacher and student sends families the message that they do not really belong at the school nor do they have significant contributions to make to their children's learning. Families of children who are struggling in school too often receive the message that the problem is the child's or the family's fault.

Dynamic teachers recognize that such tensions can create serious barriers to a child's learning and social development. But they also view the differences as a potential resource. Maggie and Don seek out undiscovered strengths and sensitivities among children—ones that can be tapped to help the child succeed. Dynamic teachers believe that, whatever the situation, families want the best for their children. Family members' inability or unwillingness to engage with teachers or other school people does not lessen Maggie's and Don's efforts to create and communicate the possibility for interaction. Maggie and Don believe that teachers can work with families as positive and valued contributors to the learning environment.

Values in Use: Reflection and Practice

Teachers' values yield messages, actions, and influence. Some teachers, however, have yet to explore or make explicit their own values and the critical role of values in working with children. Others, unfortunately, do not have the courage to act on their own values and deny them in the face of curriculum and testing demands. (We discuss this concept of professional courage in Chapter 4.) Some have difficulty imagining that a teacher's values might include responsibility for the learning and development of a special needs child, a child whose first language is not English, or a child who comes to school unprepared.

Dynamic teachers articulate their values to ever-broadening circles of colleagues and community members. These are the teachers who raise the level of conversation in the teachers' lounge beyond complaint about problems to reflection about needs and practices. Whereas other teachers may retreat into their classrooms to avoid conflict about values, dynamic teachers step forward because of their values. They are accountable to their colleagues and their communities, both admitting difficulties and searching for new perspectives and strategies.

Dynamic teachers take action, pursue new ideas and questions, talk with their colleagues, test their theories and hunches. Because they revisit their values, they question what they do and how they do it. Frequently, they pause, look at what they are doing, and realize that they need to take new directions. Because they have articulated clear values about the worth and rights of each child, they identify questions to guide their reflection in search of these new directions. The following situations were offered to us by individual dynamic teachers as dilemmas that they have faced.

Anita

Anita, a kindergarten teacher, observes Kue, a 5-year-old Cambodian boy, who comes to school in dirty clothes, occasionally has

head lice, exhibits poor social skills, and is generally treated as an out-
cast by other children. Seeing this little boy struggle in a new environment, Anita asks herself:

- How can I help this child belong?
- How can this child become a contributor to the learning in the
  classroom?
- How can I build on the strengths of this child, taking into
  account multiple intelligences and language and cultural
  differences?
- How can I involve his parents?

Anita searches for ways to include Kue. After speaking with
other parents and students from Cambodia, she incorporates some
Cambodian music and dance into the kindergarten curriculum. As
she does this, to the delight of all the students, she observes Kue
carefully for signs of interest. As the little boy begins to relate to the
other children through movement and music, Anita moves to include him in other social and academic ways.

In reflecting on her experience, Anita recalls how incorporating
Cambodian music and dance led her and the children into many
different areas for exploration, how it helped create bonds with
families, and how it helped her discover "new people" within her
group of 5-year-olds. Perhaps most important, it helped Kue become
a member of the classroom community.

Echoing Anita's experience, these briefer examples show individual students challenging teachers to reflect on their values and
practice, thereby promoting a process of inquiry and action that has
an affect on all students, not just one.

Roger

Roger, a fifth-grade teacher in an urban school, thinks about
how he can work with Carl, an unhappy, angry, disruptive 10-year-
old boy from a family suffering from poverty and problems of substance and physical abuse. Roger starts off his process of inquiry with,
How can I build on the strengths of this child? How can he become
actively involved in learning? How do I create a learning atmosphere of mutual respect and caring rather than one of control and
conflict?

Linda

Linda, a seventh-grade teacher, is concerned about Molly, a quiet 11-year-old girl showing diminishing interest in her academic work and diminishing confidence in her ability to learn and achieve. Molly's grades are sinking, and she seems to relate less and less to the other students in her class. Linda asks herself, How do I enable this child to take ownership of her learning, valuing her own interests and strengths? How do I help her feel like an insider? How can I work with her family to reverse this downward spiral? Are there other girls in the class with similar tendencies?

Al

Al, a biology teacher in a suburban high school, is thinking about Sirje, an ambitious 14-year-old girl recently arrived from a war-torn country where she had been unable to attend school for the past 4 years. She speaks little English; Al is unable to determine her language skills in her native Russian. Sirje aspires to be a physician and is anxious to begin learning content, especially biology, and is frustrated having to spend most of her time working on English skills.

Al reflects, How can I help her access the content and higher order thinking she needs? Is the textbook the only way for her to learn? Can her family be of help? Is there a classmate who could make a difference? What do her classmates understand of her situation? How would they react if they were in a similar situation? What can they do to contribute to her learning? Is there a way that she can sometimes be the expert in this class?

SUMMARY

All teachers possess values. What differentiates dynamic teachers from others is that they have articulated their values concerning children and the power of learning; they hold a particular set of values that recognizes the worth, the capabilities, and the rights of all children and their families; and they accept the responsibilities that accompany these values as they work in their schools. Dynamic teachers use their value base daily to resolve the dilemmas they encounter in establishing learning environments that balance individual and community needs and contributions. In doing so, they bring a body of knowledge to their classrooms. In the next chapter, we introduce the concept of the dynamic teacher as a constructor.

Note

1. Although we quote directly and paraphrase the words of teachers with whom we have worked, we protect their identities throughout the book.

3

The Constructor

Making Sense of Content, Pedagogy, and Development

What do dynamic teachers bring to their teaching? What is the body of knowledge they use to meet the needs of their students? What enables them to make appropriate decisions concerning student learning in the classroom? Dynamic teachers know the subject they are teaching, they are experts in pedagogy, and they know their students. Maggie and Don show the complexity of the knowledge they possess and use in their classrooms.

Don and Maggie were talking with Sonia, their student teacher, about how to integrate the study of fractions into the frontier town unit. They had agreed that Sonia would raise questions about fractions with groups in the class during the next week.

"Fractions could be part of several aspects of life in the town—baking, planting on the land, building, sewing clothes. I am sure someone will bring up how the bartender in the saloon must consider fractions as he measures his drinks!" Don laughed. "Where do you think you'll begin?"

"You two have taught me pretty well to let the children lead. I'll look over the projects this weekend and choose one where I have several questions for them about fractions."

"I'm actually glad you have responsibility for fractions this year. I always have to bone up on them before I talk to the children about them," Don said.

"What do you mean 'bone up on'? We don't have to be experts on stuff we teach, do we?" asked Sonia. "How can we? We have to cover so much!"

"Not experts, necessarily. But I find I really do need to know the subject," responded Don.

"What do you mean by 'know'?" asked Sonia.

"I have to understand it . . . to make sense of it," interjected Maggie.

"That's what I mean by 'know,' " said Don. "I construct my own meaning for it in my mind. So that I can use it in almost any form it may be presented. It—fractions or whatever—has to mean something to me."

"I know something when I can explain it to someone else. Take fractions. I have to be able to see any shape in any combination of fractions, and then I have to be able to describe what those shapes would look like," Maggie said. "Not being able to explain something to someone else is the way I realized that I really didn't know how to knit. I had to find some written directions for knitting to use when I tried to teach my daughter. Sure, I knit, but I never bothered to make sense of what really happens to the yarn when it is looped around and connected. I can only do very plain pieces . . . never cables or patterns or anything. I get confused because I don't really understand the concept. I just do it."

"Isn't that what most teachers do? Just do it? I didn't know any of my teachers had ever 'constructed their own meanings' for what they taught!" wondered Sonia. "How can we 'construct our own meanings' for everything we have to teach? That's a lot of work!"

"Did we ever tell you teaching wasn't hard work?" asked Don. "But if you understand something in the way we mean, teaching becomes easier in total. You don't have to have a script to follow—you can truly be responsive to the children and their questions. You can meet each one right where he or she is. You can be flexible. You can adapt to the unexpected."

"Like when Melissa is still groping for the words to describe what she did, whereas Roxanne is challenging the reasons for doing it?" suggested Sonia.

"Right, but we don't mean that anything goes, though," answered Maggie. "The reason we can deal with both Melissa and Roxanne is because we know what we want them to learn. And we recognize that more than one way exists to learn it."

"Part of our job is to bring knowledge to our students. So we have to know enough to be able to choose the knowledge they need," Don continued. "And kids are not empty vessels we dump knowledge into. We have to make the knowledge accessible for them. That means we have to know them, too. We have to choose strategies that will enable them to make the knowledge their own."

"You mean, they have to construct for themselves their own meanings about the knowledge," Sonia said. "As their teacher, I have to understand the knowledge myself . . . and know how to deliver it."

"I think she's got it!" cried Don.

"Elementary, my dear. Let's get back to my lessons on fractions. Now I haven't a clue where to begin."

"Tell me what a fraction is, Sonia," began Maggie.

"Fractions are parts of a whole. Sometimes they are equal, sometimes not."

"Give us an example—what does a fraction mean to you?" probed Don.

Sonia went on to describe how she got only a "fraction" of her mother's pies when she was young because she had so many brothers and sisters. She talked about how she and her friends would divide up their homework and argue about whether assignments were equal. She remembered how once she wondered how many times a piece could be halved and still exist. She had heard about half-life in radioactivity and thought she ought to explore what it might mean to her understanding of fractions. "I really do understand fractions! I am already manipulating fractions in my mind now . . . adding, subtracting, converting."

"What do the children in this class need to learn about fractions? What ideas? What skills?" asked Maggie.

"There is so much to know, even about fractions. How do I choose?"

"Don't forget, you are the professional. You have a body of knowledge—both about the subjects and about the children. You could start with what you think your students need depending on their age and abilities . . . what's in the curriculum. You need to know that stuff anyway. Where I actually begin is with the children themselves. I ask them. They tell me so much," Maggie said.

"Okay. So I need to understand the subject myself. Then I look at what the experts say. I have a sense of what I think they should learn. And I look at what the children say they want to know. What if they don't want to know anything about fractions?"

"That's where your knowledge about the subject comes in. You discover through something they are doing," Maggie told her. "Once, I gave groups in a class material and asked them to make scarves for everyone in their group. At first, I only gave them part of what they needed. We generated a lot of questions related to fractions. I found out what they did know and what they wanted to learn."

"As Don said, many activities in our frontier town use fractions. I have a good sense about fractions and what I think the children need to learn. Tomorrow, I can discover more about different children's thinking on fractions, and I can plan my activities. I'll admit, I'm more excited about teaching fractions now than I was when we began this discussion. I feel I am actually teaching!" exclaimed Sonia.

*   *   *   *   *

Maggie and Don and Sonia do more than pass on information or facts to their students. They value children and their learning. They also value the knowledge and skills they want the children to master. Although they respect their students' interpretations for what they experience in school, they equally respect the existing body of culturally accepted interpretations or symbols (Driver et al., 1994). They have reflected on and framed knowledge and skills in ways they expect will be accessible to the children. And they accept responsibility for bringing the knowledge and skills to the children. This responsibility is enormous. It is also essential for student learning. But for dynamic teachers, it is reasonable and realistic, because they are grounded in their understanding of teaching.

What Is a Constructivist Teacher?

Dynamic teachers' knowledge of the subject, of pedagogy, of their students, and of their own values concerning learning gives them a firm foundation or grounding on which to build their lessons. Before they step into their classrooms, they have constructed their own complex meanings for the subjects they have chosen to teach. Their deep understanding enables them to mold and adapt content to the needs of their particular students and to the changing contexts of the classroom. Their choice of specific topics and strategies emerges from their broad perspective of the content, as embedded in an established body of knowledge, and from their wide repertoire of teaching strategies. Furthermore, teachers like Maggie and Don know their students—their developmental stages, their individual strengths and weaknesses, their affective needs. To ensure that all their students learn, they make choices about what they will teach within the curriculum.

As Don acknowledges, being a teacher so well grounded in content and pedagogy is demanding and challenging. He also notes that it is this grounding that enables him to be responsive and flexible. He knows he needs no script or formula. He understands the principles, so if he misplaces the procedures, he can still perform; he can improvise. It is this grounding that prevents him from becoming overwhelmed by all the varied and often unpredictable demands placed on him everyday. Any teacher makes hundreds of decisions each day. The grounded teacher need not labor over every single decision and is confident that his or her decisions are principled ones.

Finally, as Maggie notes, dynamic teachers recognize that they are accountable for affording every student a valid opportunity to learn the subject. Thus they continually reflect on and inquire into the effect of their choices. Again, their foundation—their grounding in content and pedagogy—enables them to analyze and interpret the effects of their work. Although they are aware that the teaching/learning connection is not always a linear cause-and-effect relationship, they are not operating by intuition or chance. In sum, dynamic teachers like Maggie and Don are professionals in the sense that they possess a defined body of knowledge that they use to make choices in meeting the needs of the students they serve and are accountable to a high standard in meeting these needs.

Knowledge Required for Teaching

Dynamic teachers like Maggie and Don see their goal as helping students develop deep understandings, not imitating behavior. Deep understanding occurs when the presence of new information prompts the learner to rethink and reshape prior ideas (Brooks & Brooks, 1993). As teachers, they have rejected the traditional view of learning that offers discrete information and asks the learner to repeat or mime newly acquired information (Jackson, 1986). Rather, they embrace the view that learning requires the transformation and internalization of new information. They are constructivists. That is, they build their own meaning or construct for new concepts. They define knowledge as temporary and conditional, because it changes as new information is taken in; as developmental, because information is used differently as one grows; as contextually mediated, because the values and beliefs of society or culture affect understandings; and as nonobjective, because everyone's mind processes information uniquely. They understand learning as a self-regulated, ongoing process of making sense of the world through concrete experience, collaborative discourse, and reflection (Fosnot, 1993). The knowledge they bring to the classroom, therefore, is multifaceted.

This body of knowledge incorporates a deep understanding of the content area these teachers teach. Thus, Maggie and Don are themselves learners. They do not simply take information and pass it on.

They critique and shape it; they make their own sense of the material. They construct their own knowledge or meanings of the material (Duckworth, 1986; Mirman Owen, Cox, & Watkins, 1994; Rallis, 1990). But, as Maggie pointed out, not everything goes! Because cognitive abilities are specific to particular domains of knowledge (Devaney & Sykes, 1988), the teacher is an expert in the subject area; the teacher demonstrates a high level of competence and measures up to rigorous standards.

Dynamic teachers recognize that knowledge construction is not entirely an individual process. Children need access to the conventional concepts and models already accepted and shared in the culture. Each content area consists of a rich, socially constructed symbolic world; that is, a conceptually organized, rule-bound belief system about what exists and what is valued (Bruner, 1985). The dynamic teacher knows and brings the tools of this world to his or her students. In their lessons about parts and wholes, for example, Maggie and Don bring the mathematical concepts of fractions and the processes of addition and subtraction. These concepts and processes are social constructions shared in the mathematics domain (see Driver et al., 1994, for a discussion of the individual and social aspects of knowledge construction).

Theories, explanations, interpretations, problem solutions, and other ideas are not tangible objects, but once they have been accepted as part of a content area's symbolic world, they do exist. They form a discipline such as science, mathematics, or philosophy. They can be found in books and other products of scholarly activity. It is the teacher's responsibility to bring this scholarly world to the individual student's mind, where he or she may make sense of it in his or her life (see Popper, 1972, for an explication of the worlds of knowledge). A teacher, then, must understand both the scholarly world of the subject that he or she is teaching and the world inside the head of the learner.

Dynamic teachers reexamine their subject matter from a learning perspective. As teachers, their content knowledge is important only in how it can be used for students and their learning. Teachers develop "pedagogical content knowledge, . . . an understanding of what it means to teach particular subject matter to students" (Grossman & Richert, 1986, p. 3). Just as they make sense of the content knowledge, dynamic teachers make sense of learning and teaching principles so that they may apply them to their classrooms. They do not simply pour information into pupils' heads. They ask themselves, How do children learn? What do they need from me to facilitate learning? Aware of various learning theories, they construct and internalize their own theories for action. Out of these theories emerges a range of teaching strategies and techniques from which they draw.

An example of how a content area, mathematics, can be thought of from the learning perspective comes from the work of Fenema, Carpenter, Franche, and Carey (1992) on cognitively guided instruction. These researchers looked at basic mathematical operations and observed how even the youngest students could work out complex mathematical problems given certain information. They watched how a teacher's full understanding of the mathematical functions and their relationship to each other, coupled with an ability to ask a child about his or her thinking as he or she figured out a problem, allowed the teacher to guide the child to a higher level of mathematical functioning. Cognitively guided instruction presents mathematics in such a way as to help the teacher analyze how a student is constructing mathematical understanding and therefore to guide the student's growth in moving to increasingly efficient operations at increasingly more abstract levels of functioning.

Dynamic teachers recognize that learning is as natural as breathing. Believing that people are born learners, they know that all children in all classrooms are learning all the time. Often children's learnings in school are not positive, empowering concepts. Many children learn that they cannot perform or that they are not valued or that language or math or spelling is boring. The dynamic teacher works with the child to build positive learnings. The dynamic teacher creates activities that capture the child's natural curiosity and guide his or her natural learning. The goal is to enhance the child's understanding of the surrounding world and his or her relationship to it.

Drawing from Piaget and Dewey, the dynamic teacher knows that "in order to know objects, the [child] must act upon them, and therefore, transform them: he must displace, correct, combine, take them apart, and reassemble them. From the most elementary sensorimotor actions . . . to the most sophisticated intellectual operations, . . . knowledge is constantly linked with actions or operations, that is, with transformations" (Piaget, 1970a, quoted in Phillips & Soltis, 1985, p. 44). Maggie and Don also recognize that learners make sense of new information and experiences by connecting them to what they already know. Although children can often make the connections themselves, dynamic teachers take the role of helping this transfer from one context to another. Their classrooms offer children multiple opportunities to encounter new information and experiences, and their questions push students to make sense of new stimuli.

To apply their repertoire of strategies, dynamic teachers must understand their students. Their students bring varied backgrounds, stories, and languages to the classroom. Teachers like Maggie and Don view this diversity as a resource. Their constructivist minds see opportunities for students to develop richer and deeper understandings than if they were to emphasize homogeneity. Rather than assume their students fit a prescribed mold of "the typical first grader" or "the typical fifth grader," dynamic teachers assume there is no prototype. Instead, they seek to discover who their students are. They discover what their students already know in order to make choices about what questions to ask and what learning experiences to offer.

Dynamic teachers' sense of the subject becomes intertwined with their sense of their students (Macrorie, 1984). They know how their students make sense of things, what their students are curious about, what confuses them, and where their doubts lie. Their knowledge of their students comes from numerous and intimate interactions with the students and from their understanding of how people learn. This knowledge affords dynamic teachers both access and opportunity. They discover what works with one student but not with another. They discover that indirect instruction works well with students of high ability, whereas low ability learners may need more structured activities (Doyle, 1983). They choose activities to meet varied abilities and, knowing their students, they guide the students appropriately but flexibly.

Dynamic teachers also have a profound respect for the variety of ways of learning. They understand notions of "multiple intelligences" (Gardner, 1985) and the implications of this theory for classroom practice. Given that students learn in a variety of ways—linguistic or kinesthetic or spatial, for example—dynamic teachers construct multiple pathways to learning specific content for their students. They provide rich and complex learning experiences, not just those relying on linguistic skills. Furthermore, they stretch their students to learn in new ways, through media that may not be their preferred style. Thus the Maggies and Dons respect each student's particular talents but push each student into new ways of engaging with the subject matter.

Dynamic teachers also recognize the critical nature of developmental stages in children and adolescents. They have made sense of cognitive development theory, designing instructional tasks according to where they think students are developmentally, and interpreting student behavior in developmental terms. Because they understand that not all children are at the same point at the same time, they appreciate students' present constructions and help them relate to other constructions. They capitalize on developmental diversity to provide "zones of proximal development" (Vygotsky, 1978) that awaken new learning. These zones of potential learning appear as children interact with people and cooperate with peers. Dynamic teachers give children chances to watch each other, to listen to each other, to eavesdrop. Thus the children are opened to new possibilities. Again, the teacher's role is essential: To question and guide the sense students make out of the new information and experiences.

In sum, dynamic teachers like Maggie and Don are grounded teachers. They are grounded in content; they have constructed their own meaning for the material they teach. They are grounded in pedagogy; they understand how people learn. And they are grounded in their students; they understand developmental theories, and they know the children they teach. They know what turns them on, what bothers them, and what they already know. Maggie and Don and all dynamic teachers have a strong, constructed body of knowledge about children, teaching, and subject matter.

Professional Choices

In a dynamic teacher's learner-centered classroom, however, not everything goes. Dynamic teachers construct their body of knowledge, but it must be tested. It must meet defined standards, both personal and professional. The dynamic teacher holds himself or herself accountable to a personal standard based on serving the child: Is the material important to my students, and did they learn it? The dynamic teacher also holds himself or herself accountable to a professional standard: What do the principles and theories of the field say the students should learn? Am I using appropriate pedagogy? Are the students learning the material so that they can communicate it clearly to others? In short, the dynamic teacher uses professional knowledge.

Darling-Hammond (1988b) identifies three prerequisites for professional choices: (a) knowledge of principles, theories, and factors undergirding decisions about what procedures should be employed—and knowledge of the procedures themselves; (b) the ability to apply this knowledge in nonroutine circumstances; and (c) a commitment to do what is judged best for the client. The primary basis of professionalism is the application of knowledge to serve a client. Dynamic teachers do exactly that. They do not follow directives blindly; they do not simply adapt curriculum; they are not satisfied with end-of-unit testing. Rather, they make choices to meet the needs of their students, and they assess the effect of their choices according to how the students use what they offer. Their expertise gives them freedom to choose.

Dynamic teachers' decisions can be guided by standards set by colleagues in professional associations such as the National Council of Teachers of Mathematics Curriculum and Evaluation Standards for School Mathematics (1989) and the Professional Standards for Teaching Mathematics (National Council of Teachers of Mathematics, 1991). These standards aim to delineate the accepted symbolic constructs for each professional culture. The profession as a group is responsible for defining, transmitting, and enforcing professional standards. But ultimately, whether a profession agrees upon an acceptable common standard or not, dynamic teachers hold themselves accountable to a standard they draw from their own body of knowledge and its use for their students. Their responsibility is allocated according to their expertise, not their role (see Darling-Hammond, 1988a, for further discussion). Their knowledge gives them the authority to control their own agendas. The dynamic teacher is responsible for building his or her knowledge base and for reviewing his or her own practice through self-evaluation (Rallis, 1988).

Maggie and Don, for example, choose to teach fractions because they believe fractions are a part of life and that children need to understand and use them to be successful. They help Sonia make explicit her own understanding of fractions in order to make choices about how she will teach them to her class. She makes decisions about content and strategies based on her sense of the subject, her students, and available procedures. After working with the students on fractions, Sonia will observe their use of fractions and listen to their understandings, assessing their ability to communicate their learnings. For those students who cannot communicate an understanding of fractions, she will choose other procedures. For those students who communicate an understanding that does not match the accepted principles and theories about fractions, Sonia will choose another strategy. Her goal is to enable students to build constructs that connect with others and to communicate these constructs.

For dynamic teachers, teaching is much more than skilled transmission; it is principled action. Dynamic teachers internalize principles for deciding what to teach when and how. "Teaching involves a process calling for intuition, creativity, improvisation, and expressiveness, and it leaves room for departures from what is implied by rules and formulae" (Devaney & Sykes, 1988, p. 6). Shulman (1987) reminds us that the teacher's knowledge is not fixed; it is discovered, invented, and refined. Teachers' choices must fit within district and state frameworks, but their judgment about what motivates particular students to learn is the main determinant of the educational program. This judgment is grounded in the teachers' knowledge.

Becoming a Grounded Teacher

Although they have always valued children's learning, Maggie and Don developed their grounding over the years, beginning with their college training. They continued it, often seeking professional development, both informally and formally, sometimes pursuing advanced degrees. They interact with colleagues, both inside and outside the school, in districtwide meetings and at conferences and workshops. They participate in projects that draw on their practical knowledge and build their theoretical knowledge. Above all, they are teacher-researchers; that is, they inquire into their practice (Duckworth, 1986; Miller, 1990; Uhl, Perez-Selles, & Rallis, 1995). For each lesson, they conduct mini action research studies where they ask, What are we expecting students to learn from this experience? What are the students doing differently? What do we see the students learning? Maggie and Don also serve as mentors for Sonia. Thus they are teachers creating knowledge within their practice (Loucks-Horsley, in press).

Dynamic teachers acknowledge that they are learners themselves. Their learning is developmental, in which peers play an important role. Collaboration stimulates and renews their interest and builds confidence. Just as their children benefit from working next to peers who are at different levels (Cummings, 1981; Kerr & Slocum, 1981; Vygotsky, 1978), dynamic teachers learn from colleagues. Loucks-Horsley (in press; see also Sparks, 1994) describes learner-centered schools as places that simultaneously require and bring with them a new paradigm for professional development. In this new paradigm, learning is embedded in the job and is considered essential. Dynamic teachers not only thrive in this setting, they also contribute to it.

Grounded Teachers in Action

As Don points out, being a grounded teacher is both demanding and rewarding. Teachers like Maggie and Don work hard to build their knowledge bases to make principled choices, but they also have freedom. Because they act on principles, they can be creative and are not overwhelmed by immense tasks they face daily. Because they carry in their minds their own constructs for what they teach, they can adapt to unanticipated situations. Their lessons become their own.

Fran and Robin

Fran and Robin team teach fifth grade in a small middle school. One of their favorite units is nutrition. Over their years of teaching the unit, they have sought to construct a meaningful experience around which to engage their classes. Fran has a strong background in nutrition studies; both teachers understand the range of developmental needs of their fifth graders; both possess a repertoire of instructional strategies.

Robin observed that several of the female students had developed eating disorders and believed that preadolescents desperately needed to build their own definition of what it means to "eat well." Several years ago Fran and Robin designed a game around the four food groups. Students loved playing the game, so they formalized the rules. Playing the game became an event students looked forward to as they entered the school. As the food groups turned into the food pyramid, and as Fran's and Robin's knowledge about nutrition and about teaching grew, they revised the game to better meet the needs of those they were teaching. Now, every year after playing the game with their classes, they review the interactions and learnings. They make revisions. Teaching nutrition is, for them, an ongoing process where they learn as well as the students. They are grounded teachers.

Carmen

Carmen teaches first grade using an integrated curriculum. She begins each unit asking the children the questions they have about the topic. "I used to think I needed to know all the answers. Now, I realize that if I really know the subject, I know I don't know all the answers, can never know all the answers. We study the rain forest. We ask questions. We gather information. We visit the rain forest with the questions in mind. So, cada año aprendo más acerca del bosque tropical [each year we learn more about the rain forest]. We always leave with more questions. We know there is more to learn because of the trees and the animals. Each day is different. My knowledge is where to begin and where to go with these children." Carmen is comfortable in her uncertainty because she is a grounded teacher.

Cheryl

Cheryl teaches in a multiage classroom. "We had to move to multiage because we knew our kids. We saw that one grade and one curriculum were missing the mark for about half of them. People ask me if it is harder, but I see it as giving me more freedom to choose what is best for each kid. No, I don't have 30 different lesson plans every day. Children are doing different things, but it all fits together within the topic area. I know the topic, and I can try lots of different ways to teach it. The part I find I spend more time on is assessment. I really have to be sure they get what I think they have!"

SUMMARY

Dynamic teachers value learning and knowledge. They consciously construct their own meanings for information and experiences based on their deep awareness of existing social constructions. They share those constructs with colleagues for scrutiny and critique. Above all, dynamic teachers value their students' learning. They know that each child learns in a somewhat different way than any other. They also know that more than one pathway exists to learning anything. The knowledge dynamic teachers bring to their students helps them on their varied pathways to learning.

Dynamic teachers are grounded in their knowledge. They deeply understand their subjects, their pedagogy, and their children. This knowledge is a part of their lives. But with the knowledge comes a responsibility. As teachers, they must bring experiences and information to students to build into their own knowledge. They must not prescribe or limit students' interpretations or use of the experiences or information. They know learning and knowledge are not finite commodities with start and end points. As professionals, these teachers make choices based on their knowledge. They take actions and then reflect on those actions; they hold themselves accountable. They are experts, and they accept the responsibility that comes with the freedom to make choices.

Undergirding dynamic teachers' knowledge and skills in content, pedagogy, and their students is a deep sense of professional commitment to their work. This commitment is visible in the ways they think about their work, the actions taken within their classrooms to further students' learning, and how they hold themselves accountable. This philosophy is described more fully in the next chapter.

4

The Philosopher

Using Professional
Commitment to Make a Difference

*Dynamic teachers approach their work with articulated values,
extensive knowledge, and solid pedagogy. What glue binds these
facets into dynamic practice? How do dynamic teachers use these
elements to make a difference in their professional lives? Maggie
and Don reveal their philosophy of professional commitment.*

As the winter neared, Maggie and Don became frustrated with the students' engagement in the frontier town project. They were unsure about its direction and felt that the adopt-a-shop idea was not working well. Although a handful of students had visited their selected "shops," several had not.

"What do we need to do to move this adopt-a-shop idea along?" Maggie asked Don over coffee early one morning.

"Tell me what's bugging you about it," Don probed.

"I'm not sure. . . . It just isn't taking off the way we thought. And I don't know what to do. . . . I'm stuck." Maggie looked at Don hopefully. He always seemed able to get her and the students "unstuck" when they were spinning their wheels.

"Let's talk about it some more," Don encouraged her.

Maggie felt a burden lift, as if she didn't have to have all the answers; she could just let the ideas out and see where they went. What a great colleague Don was!

"Well, three of the kids have visited a shop. Ling Pao, of course, because of her dad's grocery store. Joey went to his neighbor's, Patrick Reilly's, shoe repair place. Carlos went to the Mexican fast-food place—Juanita's, I think it's called. But I don't think any of the others have made a move . . . and it worries me. Maybe we need to be more structured: Give them a set of questions to ask, something like that."

After a moment's silence, Don asked Maggie if this was really what she wanted to do.

"No, of course not!" Maggie exclaimed in exasperation. "But sometimes it's so hard to figure out how to get things moving. And I feel torn between letting the kids take the lead and maybe not getting to a local store and us directing them. *We* know the experience could be rich!"

"Let's think back over what we hoped would happen with this adopt-a-shop idea. What were we thinking? How did we envision the experience unfolding?" Don pushed Maggie and himself to reflect back on their original notion.

Maggie offered the following: "I think we wanted them to learn about the shops in the community and relate that to the shops that were in frontier towns: What is the same? What is different? Why? How has the economy changed? Things like that. And we wanted them to see the ways other people serve the community—what they bring to the area, what they offer . . . what it could be like without them."

"You know that we're trying to build more democratic processes in the classroom, ones where the kids get to participate in important decisions. Maggie, think about how well the morning meeting is going: how they participate, make decisions, share ideas with each other. What would you think about putting this on the morning meeting agenda today? Ask the kids what's working and what isn't and why not. Get them to tell us what the problems are and what might work better for them. What do you think?" Don asked Maggie thoughtfully.

"Great idea!" Maggie felt better already! She had a colleague who could help determine a direction. . . . No, Don didn't have all the answers, but he reminded her that the kids probably did . . . they were the place to go!

Morning meeting focused on this important aspect of the frontier town project. Maggie and Don described to the students the problems they saw with the adopt-a-shop idea; they "disarmed" the students and said, in effect, this isn't working well and we need you to help us understand why not. The students were eloquent about their fears about walking into a store, not knowing whom to approach, feeling self-conscious, not being sure what they wanted to accomplish. Maggie and Don felt a bit chagrined: They should have known all this! But the students were marvelous in articulating the difficulties they were having.

Together Maggie, Don, and the students redirected this aspect of the project. Some students had easy access to stores, others did not. Some felt comfortable reaching out "solo" to a store owner; others wanted to do this in pairs or in a small group. The class, working together, redesigned the adopt-a-shop element of the frontier town project to draw on community resources in ways that respected the students' different strengths.

*   *   *   *   *

Thus far, we have described dynamic teachers who have the potential to change dramatically the experience of schooling for children, and we have reflected on what these teachers bring to today's schools. We have explored their values and guiding principles, as well as their understanding of how people learn, their extensive knowledge and skills, and their active approach to learning. In this chapter, we discuss how these values and knowledge are enacted in practice, expressing a philosophy of professional commitment.

Professional Commitment:
A Philosophy for Action

What do we mean by professional commitment? Quite simply, we mean courage—the courage to learn, the courage to act, the courage to reflect on those actions critically, and the courage to be accountable for those actions. This commitment ensures that teachers will continue to grow professionally to serve children, the community, and society better. Our purpose in this chapter is to describe the messy, interactive elements of professional commitment: taking initiative and acting; reflecting on and critically inquiring about values, knowledge, and actions; and being responsible and accountable for both processes and outcomes for the self and students. Undergirding these actions are the dynamic teacher's values, guiding principles, knowledge, and skills. Taken together, these form what we call a "philosophy of professional commitment."

Maggie and Don reveal the elements of this philosophy in the previous vignette. Their purpose is to secure what is desired and desirable, based on their values and knowledge, through action, inquiry, and thought. They use their intelligence to achieve this purpose by thinking about what they do before, during, and after they do it. They are unflinching in their assessment of what works and what does not work in the classroom; they reflect critically on what is happening; they take initiative and act, making midcourse corrections as necessary; and they are profoundly responsible for their actions and for what happens in the classroom.

Dynamic teachers follow no recipes or models; rather, they constantly attend to what they are doing with an eye on their goal and on inventing new ways to accomplish it. Through experience, they evolve their own knowledge of how to be a good teacher.

> Teaching is always a becoming. To paraphrase Dewey's definition of growth, teaching for the [dynamic] teacher is the constant reorganization, reconstruction, and transformation of one's experience. It is developing one's *philosophy* of teaching and of education as well. And, to paraphrase William James, one's philosophy must make a definite difference in the way one lives his or her professional life. (Soltis, 1994, p. 253, emphasis added)

If we understand a philosophy as a set of principles and assumptions that guides a person's life, the dynamic teacher's daily professional life expresses this complex mix of values and knowledge, action and thought—the philosophy of professional commitment.

The elements of this philosophy are neither linear nor sequential; they form a seamless web of *praxis* (Freire, 1970)—the blending of theory and practice. These elements interact in richly textured ways; in this chapter, we focus on the facets of practice where the philosophy becomes visible. These facets reveal the extraordinary capabilities of dynamic teachers.

Kolb (1984) describes experiential learning as an interactive learning and problem-solving process that requires (a) observing concrete experiences, (b) reflecting on and questioning why things are happening, (c) drawing from other sources to add new thinking, and (d) developing a plan and taking action. These aspects are indivisible for effective learning: One observes and questions while acting; gathers new information and resources while reflecting; and so on. One process may be in the foreground while the others are in the background. To Kolb's model, we add the moral dimensions of teaching: being responsible and accountable to oneself, students, the community, the profession, and the wider society.

These elements blur together in an iterative process of professional growth and revitalization that is transformational for teacher, learning environment, and student. Several concepts come to mind: double-loop learning or meta-cognitive processes, for example. Another image that helps convey what we mean is the multitasking capabilities of the modern generation of personal computers. Dynamic teachers engage in multiple, highly complex tasks at any given point in time. As they experiment with new methods for reaching a student, they put new knowledge into practice, reflecting on the ways this fits their emergent understandings of learning and critically judging—being responsible for—the learning event's usefulness in helping one child learn. Dynamic teachers are, moreover, willing to subject their practice to scrutiny; they are accountable for their actions.

We have struggled with a metaphor to capture this philosophy, finally choosing a musical one.[1] The philosophy of professional commitment is substantially shaped and determined by the dynamic teacher's values and knowledge—these are captured by the key and time signature of a piece of music. Within these boundaries, the rich interplay of melody and harmonics symbolizes the disciplined, artistic

Figure 4.1. The Philosophy of Professional Commitment.

expression that captures the dynamic teacher's practice. We envision the interacting elements as shown in Figure 4.1

We see this philosophy as a rich, textured piece of music that dynamic teachers play in all aspects of their work. Their actions express both deeply held values about education and more concrete knowledge and skills. As they journey toward increasing professional growth, dynamic teachers inquire and reflect, take initiative and act, and accept responsibility and are accountable for their own and their students' learning. All these elements merge in the various roles dynamic teachers enact, described in the chapters to follow. Teachers move through this score over and over again, playing at one time the violin, at another the piano.

Most of all, this performance requires courage. These processes—these frames of mind—are by no means easy or undemanding; they go beyond what many of today's teachers would accept as professional commitment. We believe, however, that many creative and ethical teachers have the courage and energy to be willing to revisit their values and aspirations, and their practice.

Professional commitment entails teachers' dedication to their professional growth and development as teachers, learners, and advocates for children. Dynamic teachers realize that each day with children brings new challenges. Their vision for a particular day, month, or year may be clear, but actual practice is exquisitely sensitive to the emergent needs and strengths of the learners in the classroom. Thus, even within the constraints of a musical composition, there is room for modification, adaptation—improvisation.

Dynamic teachers understand that, to respond to these emergent needs and to bring fresh insights to the classroom, they should be lifelong learners. They recognize that their knowledge and skills will stagnate unless they are enriched by their own growth. Thus, dynamic teachers think of themselves as learners, along with the children in their classrooms. For them, teaching and learning are inseparable acts.

Meaningful commitment to children in schools today requires the courage to think, act, reflect, and be accountable in ways that may be uncomfortable. More often than not, teachers struggle alone to learn and improve their practice. Dynamic teachers, however, reach out to learn collaboratively. Their learning draws from their relationships with children, colleagues, and others in the community (Soltis, 1994). We see Maggie learning through conversation both with Don and with her students. The conversations generate questions and new perspectives, as well as answers.

The following sections explicate the three elements of professional commitment that dynamic teachers model in their schools every day. These elements, although distinctive parts, are integrated into a whole philosophy. In musical performance, individual instruments —at times playing together, at other times playing solo—bring a score to life, just as the dynamic teacher's values come to life through action, reflection, and thought.

Values as Guiding Principles

As explained in Chapters 2 and 3, the work and interactions of dynamic teachers are driven by deeply held values about children, families, and the responsibilities of teachers, as well as a constantly growing understanding of how people learn, learn best, and learn differently. These make up the background from which teachers build, remodel, and rebuild the way they enact their profession.

The teacher returns to this foundation when faced with the increasingly difficult and complex needs of students and the changing demands of society. Dynamic teachers do not allow this foundation to become weak through neglect. Rather, they stay keenly aware of their values by revisiting them, making new connections, reflecting on and questioning them, and checking for congruence between values and actions. They use them as a wellspring for their courage when required to stand up for what they believe or to justify their actions. Dynamic teachers, moreover, search for new knowledge and practice new skills to enhance their core understandings. One strategy to keep alive this value system and the knowledge and skills that guide practice is to inquire and reflect. Another is to take initiative and action. Interwoven with both are a profound sense of responsibility and accountability.

Initiative and Action

Values and principles informed by knowledge of learning and skills in teaching are expressed in daily practice: the mundane, exciting, frustrating, joyful life of classrooms and schools. Through their practice, dynamic teachers' philosophy becomes visible. In the classroom, we see the suppleness, flexibility, confidence, and courage that make these teachers superb professionals. Like well-trained musicians, dynamic teachers are confident in their knowledge and skills and sure in a vision of where they are going, just as they are dedicated to examining critically what happens in the classroom and making midcourse modifications to ensure that all students learn.

Professional commitment requires action. Inquiry and reflection without action become hollow promises. Dynamic teachers take initiative . . . sometimes boldly, sometimes cautiously. But they have the courage to act—to change their practice to serve students better. We offer three illustrations of teachers in schools demonstrating their professional commitments. The first vignette portrays a teacher striving to meet the complex needs of a student with substantial disabilities. The teacher observes, reflects, critically examines his practice with the help of valued peers, reaches out to the family, and implements some new practices to foster the child's growth. The next two vignettes show teams of teachers acting out their professional commitments together.

Megan and Basketball

Ron teaches second grade in a small, rural elementary school. Megan has attended this school since her preschool days and is well-known to students and staff alike. A loving child, Megan has substantial cognitive delays—by age 9, she can repeat some words in sentence-like format—but communicates quite well nonverbally with both staff and peers. Although Ron is an experienced teacher, he has been stymied by Megan's apparent lack of growth in language acquisition.

Ron has been in close consultation with the specialist teacher and Megan's one-on-one paraprofessional about her needs. All three feel that Megan's language skills could show growth if they could touch her through something that matters a great deal to her. Because she cannot articulate what that might be, the teachers feel at a loss. Discussions with the family have been difficult, moreover, because Megan's father works at a local high-tech company and is not available during school hours and her mother works the night shift as a registered nurse and has to sleep while Megan attends school.

Ron questions his own work with Megan during the first few months of the year, then decides to seek help from a veteran colleague who is a neighbor of Megan's family. They reflect together, share observations about the child and the family, and explore possible strategies to enable Megan's growth. Ron tries out some new approaches the following week, only to have Megan erupt time and again in frustration.

One Monday, after a particularly trying day with Megan, Ron arrives home to a message from his colleague. The colleague's voice is filled with excitement as he relates that he saw Megan at the basketball hoop in her driveway over the weekend. With great persistence, she threw the ball time and again, trying to make a basket. The colleague went over and chatted with Megan and her father, who confirmed that Megan had become dedicated to the basketball hoop!

Armed with this knowledge, Ron renews his commitment to talking directly with Megan's parents. He arranges to visit their home the next Thursday evening during the brief half-hour when both parents are home. A long conversation is not possible, but Ron does learn from the father that Megan became fascinated with a college basketball game on television, found an old ball in the garage, and has spent nearly every spare minute practicing. Perhaps this is the key to helping Megan.

Ron now has new knowledge and potential resources to reach out to Megan. He plans over the weekend and, early Monday morning, decorates a bulletin board with photographs of basketball players. With several new ideas and approaches, Ron takes action and begins to have limited success in helping Megan articulate more complex words. Sharing these approaches and their results—both the successes and the flops—with the specialist and paraprofessional, he feels a renewed sense of efficacy in reaching one small girl. He further realizes that his knowledge of her particular challenges is very limited, and at a faculty meeting he suggests that all the "regular" teachers could benefit from sustained in-service work on the needs of children with substantial language disabilities. He and three others form a study group that will research available resources in the area and report back to the full faculty.

Ron's story shows us how a dynamic teacher observes, reflects, reaches out to colleagues and the family, tries out small-scale experiments, reflects again, makes modifications, tries these out, and judges their effectiveness, in a continual process to meet one child's needs better. Although the mark of dynamic teachers is in the progress and growth of their students, often the scope of their professional commitment moves beyond the classroom; dynamic teachers often take initiative and action on the school and community levels. The Rainbow Project illustrates such reaching out to the community.

The Rainbow Project

Hillside is a rural school serving a population that is economically impoverished but generally supportive of the school. A sense of community—both within the school and with the town—however, had been minimal over the years, and the teachers were concerned about it. A team of five teachers had been attending a study group on community facilitated by a local educational service organization. During their first year of participation, the teachers had read widely about fostering community in schools, but many specific practices did not seem to suit their unique circumstances until they learned of a school in a neighboring state that had restructured its student groups into multiage teams and begun a community outreach initiative. They scheduled a visit. Five teachers went and learned about this exciting effort to improve the learning environment and to involve the community more fully in the school. Following the visit, the teachers started a Design Team to plan and implement multiage teams at Hillside.

Planning sessions with teachers, students, and community members ensued over the next year. The Design Team sought advice from consultants and other colleagues. When we visited Hillside one Friday in November, we attended the school's assembly, to which students wear the color of their team. A sea of red, blue, white, and green shirts greeted us as we entered the multipurpose room. The first activity was singing the Rainbow song, composed by the school's music teacher. Chills ran down our spines as the young voices rang out. Afterwards, a second-grade teacher shared a copy of the local newspaper. The headline article, written by a parent, featured the school's Rainbow Project and its commitment to honoring the diversity within the school and community. This project was originally conceived as a way to facilitate cohesion within the school by recognizing and celebrating diversity in students and staff. After three years, it has grown to include families and community members so that they may participate in the life of the school in positive ways.

The Hillside vignette shows us a committed group of dynamic teachers who have dedicated themselves to learning, reflecting, and acting. They are willing to visit other schools and learn from them; they do not dismiss successful practice as impossible. And they show the perseverance to engage in the difficult work of planning, hearing diverse voices, forging a consensus, and restructuring their school. All agree that the teams foster more respect among students, an honoring of diverse student strengths, and a greater spirit of commitment to the school. Teachers at Hillside are not complacent, however, as they plan initiatives to involve the community further in the daily life of the school. One strategy, introduced in the fall, is to place displays of student work in the town library, inviting those interested to visit whenever they like. A small-scale experiment such as this can reap powerful benefits for the students at Hillside. In PS 44 we present another example of dynamic teachers reaching out to the community, this time through their students.

Empowering Students

Public School 44 serves a largely low income area and faces multiple challenges in meeting the needs of its students. Many come to school hungry; others face abusive family situations when they return home at the end of the day; some have mild learning challenges that require flexible and individualized approaches in the classroom. The state has recently mandated site-based management to encourage schools to explore their unique strengths and to foster greater community participation.

Formed the previous year in anticipation of the state mandate, PS 44's school council comprises teachers, the principal, community representatives, and a business partner. During the year, several teachers became disenchanted with the work of the council, noting that students were visibly absent from the discussion. One dynamic professional, a social worker assigned to the school, urged the council members to invite student participation. Begun in the fall, student membership on the council has resulted in an impressive initiative.

As the council revisited its mission, participants realized that they needed a fuller assessment of community needs and interests. Taking this on as a project, the student members designed and conducted a survey of the entire community. Because the students felt personally responsible for and committed to the survey's success, the survey had an unusually high return rate.

Reflections have begun on the information gathered through the survey, with student and community members acting as the "litmus test" of the value of suggestions. As PS 44 rewrites its mission statement, it is on surer ground because of the participation of students and their highly effective survey of the community.

From PS 44 we learn of teachers asking critical questions about the school council: Why is this not working as well as we had hoped? Where are the voices of students? Why are they excluded? These are difficult questions that challenge the status quo in many schools. Once voiced, however, these questions were considered and acted on: Students became full members of the council with the unanticipated benefit of their taking responsibility for the survey of their community. The dynamic faculty and staff on this council were open to new possibilities, willing to rethink the often taken-for-granted status of students, and, above all, to act in the best interests of the students, the school, and the community it serves. Their actions informed their inquiry.

Reflection and Inquiry: Asking Critical Questions

Reflection and inquiry are essential tools for learning; they are processes that build on one's own experiences, coupled with insights gained from others. Reflection and questioning are crucial to professional commitment, actions that are often lost in the busy lives of teachers. We emphasize this element because it is the one most often overlooked.

As dynamic teachers mediate ideas, construct meaning and knowledge, and act, they conduct inquiry. They question their assumptions and are consciously thoughtful about their goals, practices, students, and contexts (Richardson, 1994). They collect data systematically as a source of insight into their own professional practice (Clift, Veal, Johnson, & Holland, 1990). When shared, these insights often prove useful to colleagues. Their purpose is to improve practice.

Dynamic teachers share a critically important perspective: They have taken a "reflective turn" (Schon, 1991). They attempt to give their practice reason (Bamberger & Duckworth, 1982): They observe, describe, and try to illuminate what is actually done in their classrooms. They explore the patterns of activity that make up their practice. When the patterns appear unusual or puzzling, they try to make sense of the situation. Sometimes their reflections lead them to reassess the sense they have made of the overall pattern. In sum, they question and discover understandings built into their practice.

The teachers we have seen and learned from demonstrate that they are actively learning, thinking, changing, and growing. Sometimes, they find discoveries in what they already know how to do. Often, they reach out for new opportunities or create them either alone or with colleagues. With a firm sense of their values and humility about their knowledge and skills, dynamic teachers think about and question what they do and why —they inquire about their practice. Their inquiry focuses on deep values, specific knowledge, and everyday actions.

Inquiry entails asking critical questions, searching for new information, and reflecting on what is happening in the classroom and school. Dynamic teachers closely observe; they pay attention to events as they unfold and connect them to their vision of a child's learning. How are the students participating in the lesson? What initiative are they taking for shaping the work? Is the subject matter relevant and authentic? Which children need more practice asking questions? Dynamic teachers identify new areas for focus: How can the girls become more involved in science thinking? What chemistry would be appropriate and motivating for fourth graders?

The processes of inquiry and reflection need not be conducted alone. For many dynamic teachers, inquiry and reflection mean reaching out, observing what others do, listening to what others say, discussing, disputing. It means hearing and carefully considering others' opinions. It may mean sharing concerns, struggles, and frustrations, as well as insights, ideas, and innovations. Dynamic teachers open themselves up for critique and welcome new perspectives and feedback.

This inquiry can encompass asking family members of students about what they want most from their child's education, what they see as their child's strengths, or what worries them. Dynamic teachers try to reflect with families about what is best for each individual child in school. In addition, in the context of school councils, dynamic teachers reflect with other teachers, administrators, families, and community members about the school's mission and goals. With these important stakeholders, dynamic teachers seriously consider what children really need to learn. They also interact with people and resources beyond the immediate school community with whom they have contact through grants and projects, college and university courses, staff development activities, and other professional experiences.

The following two vignettes depict teachers inquiring about how they and their schools can better meet students' needs.

John and Pedra

John is among a group of teachers embarking on the development of their own professional teacher portfolios. Within these portfolios, the teachers hope to demonstrate and document what they believe, what they do, and the effect of what they do, especially their effect on their students' learning. John's first entry is what he calls his philosophy of education. He asked two of his colleagues to read his statement and critique it in light of several activities he included in the folder. He welcomed their assessment. John asked, Does my practice match my philosophy? Does it help all my students make sense of the material? How can I improve my work? One colleague asked John to explain and offered interpretations. The other colleague suggested ways John could frame the philosophy and activities as a communication with families. John remarked on the value of these reflections, done in a context of trust.

Pedra, another teacher, finds the portfolio process threatening. Although she is able to articulate the importance of students engaging in self-assessment, she sees no value in reflecting about her own work. About teacher inquiry, she asks, "But why would an adult want to do that?" She does not see changes in her work as a positive turn, and she cannot imagine her peers making judgments about her work in a noncompetitive context.

Jerri

Thurman is a community school located in a troubled urban area: Crack cocaine dealers frequent the street corner across from the school, children walking home are not safe, iron bars across windows indicate a high crime rate. Many children return home to care for younger siblings or to be cared for themselves by an aunt or older sibling. Food is neither plentiful nor assured; many students receive free lunches in the school's cafeteria.

Because of changes in the use of school space, teachers feel they might need to change the process for bringing the children into their classrooms in the morning. The current system is controlling and structured, with age groups strictly separated and children required to stand up tall in straight lines in silence. One teacher, Jerri, has heard that a neighboring school, Vibrant Springs, has a different way of managing the "morning lineup" and has arranged to visit that school with a colleague and a parent who is also a paraprofessional.

The primary purpose of this visit is to observe the morning procedure and decide whether it would work at Thurman. The criteria for success have already been set; the procedure must answer these questions: Does it ensure safety? Does it prevent disruptive behavior? Is it efficient in getting children to class? Jerri's two companions immediately note that the lines of children are not straight and that some children are sitting on the floor talking to one another. Both express concerns about the noise level. They doubt that Vibrant Springs' morning process would work at Thurman. Jerri, the inquiring teacher, sees much more. Not only is she open enough to believe she can see possibilities in another school, but she asks the recurring question, "What is best for the students?"

The alternative morning procedure interests Jerri because it expands her view of the way things could be. She discovers at Vibrant Springs an atmosphere that is different from Thurman's—a difference she could feel the minute she entered the building. In this brief visit, Jerri notes that the children seem much more comfortable than in her own school. They talk with each other in groups of mixed ages. Teachers talk with each other and with children. Family members also move in and out of conversations. She notices respectful interactions without undertones of control. The halls are noisy but in no way out of control or unsafe. She observes nothing that she would describe as disruptive or violent.

Later that day, Jerri asks herself, as do her two colleagues, "Could such a morning procedure work in Thurman?" But unlike her colleagues, Jerri does not dismiss Vibrant Springs's practice because it does not conform to Thurman's standards of straight lines and silence. Instead, her inquiry reaches beyond to deeper issues about the school, wondering about the deeply held values of Vibrant Springs and how these are embedded in such an everyday occurrence as the morning routine. She ponders some of the following questions:

- What has created this comfortable atmosphere for children and adults?
- How have teachers and students created a school where children of all ages and adults carry on informal conversations together?
- How do the principal's attitudes about and expectations for student behavior influence the atmosphere of the school?
- If students in my school were able to have a more natural beginning to their school day, would fewer discipline problems erupt?
- How could we experiment with new procedures?

When faced with the need for a new morning process at school, Jerri is open enough to reach outside for possible answers. She shows confidence in her observational abilities and is not afraid to question her school's practice. She demonstrates the courage to question, to reflect, to discover. Jerri shows us that change does not occur in a vacuum: Thinking about changing the morning routine stimulates thoughts about the culture of the school, student behavior, administrative practice, and relationships between students and teachers.

Asking critical questions and reflecting on practice, however, are not enough—dynamic teachers take action. They conduct what might be called "small-scale experiments" to test out new ideas. This then stimulates more observation, inquiry, and reflection, as they seek to create learning environments that better meet the needs and strengths of their students. They consider the effects of the experiments, the practice, and their roles in how actions have unfolded. And so the complex process continues.

Responsibility and Accountability

Dynamic teachers take responsibility and hold themselves and their colleagues accountable—they are ethical professionals. If they judge their actions as not achieving their purposes and vision, they have the courage to change their actions. The lessons that do not quite work or seem to go astray are their responsibility, not someone else's. They articulate the reasons behind their actions and redirect the actions as necessary. And they advocate the interests of children through their actions as much as their words.

The philosophy of professional commitment entails the courage to continuously revisit one's knowledge base through action and inquiry, thereby demonstrating a sense of responsibility to children, their families, the profession, and, ultimately, the wider society. As Darling-Hammond (1988a) notes, part of being a professional is to examine one's knowledge and practice critically. Is my knowledge base current and complete? Does it incorporate the most recent thinking in my field? Are my interpretations congruent with accepted understandings? Does my practice reflect this thinking? Critical examination of one's knowledge is one standard of ethical practice.

Another is to use that knowledge to serve the client responsibly. If critical examination of one's knowledge entails "continual learning [and] reflection," then ensuring that one is serving the client responsibly constitutes a "concern with the multiple effects of one's actions" (Darling-Hammond, 1988a, p. 39). Thus, the dynamic teacher asks, Are my students' best interests being served through my practice? Are there ways I could modify what happens in the classroom to better meet students' needs and strengths? Are my actions having the desired results?

Dynamic teachers, being responsible professionals, engage in reasoned experiments; they do not try things out capriciously. After visiting Vibrant Springs, Jerri does not return to Thurman and urge that her colleagues adopt Vibrant Springs's model wholesale. Instead, she reflects on her knowledge about Thurman, incorporating what she has learned at Vibrant Springs. She tests out what might work, what might not . . . she synthesizes her new knowledge with the old, reconceptualizing possibilities for her, and the school's, practice. Her actions indicate that she is learning from Vibrant Springs, but she takes the time to reflect on her existing knowledge about Thurman, sound ethical practice, and the needs and strengths of the children she serves.

Jerri feels a powerful sense of responsibility to improve the morning procedures for students. Struck with the overall atmosphere at Vibrant Springs, her initial questions lead her to examine the very core of her own school. Such critical questioning and reflecting are driven by deep concerns about the disrespectful, often disruptive, behavior by students and teachers alike that she has witnessed at Thurman. She feels professionally responsible for what has become an unworkable situation.

Jerri's responsible use of her knowledge is evident in her capacities to make judgments about possible new practices that have promise for her school—a kind of initial screening. Then she reflects on what knowledge she already possesses that will enable her to judge whether a new practice will work at Thurman. This is an integrative process, rather than merely additive. That is, Jerri blends her new experiences with existing knowledge to reconceptualize her understandings of Thurman as a school and its morning routine practice. She searches to find actions that express moral values and professional ethics. We see Jerri as the constructivist, creating a new understanding of Thurman based on her inquiry conducted at Vibrant Springs. Thus dynamic teachers are thoughtful, careful, and ethical—they are responsible—in taking action.

Dynamic teachers also hold themselves and their colleagues accountable for their actions and for the results of those actions. They are willing to display their practice and the work of their students to their colleagues' scrutiny, as well as to the scrutiny of those with vested interests in schooling: families, the community, state agencies, and policymakers. Dynamic teachers are willing, moreover, to display the operating procedures of the school—its practice—to those same groups. Thus their practice does not occur in isolation; they understand that, as moral stewards, they hold a sacred trust—the growth and development of society's children.

SUMMARY

Maggie and Don use each other to examine and improve their practice. Using their values and knowledge and skills as a base, they inquire into their practice, taking initiative and assuming responsibility for their actions. They are accountable. Their ultimate goal is to improve their practice to make their classrooms better places for the children who learn in them. They are guided by a philosophy of professional commitment that is grounded in their values and knowledge and expressed in their actions, reflection, and accountability.

To return to our musical metaphor, we understand this philosophy as a highly complex piece of music with dynamic teachers the composers, musicians, and audience. They possess the disciplined skills and knowledge to create and play the piece, as well as the capacities of *connoisseurship* and *criticism* for this "so delicate a performance as teaching" (Eisner, 1991, p. 6). They have the knowledge, skills, and creativity to compose a richly evocative and meaningful score. Like fine symphony orchestra members, they are highly trained and skilled in its performance. And they bring to their work the exquisite sensibilities of appreciation: They are able to see, not just look, and can "illuminate a situation" (Eisner, 1991, p. 6) so its meaning and value can be understood. Although some composers might shudder at the possibility, dynamic teachers improvise in their performance. As they appreciate and critique their work, they adapt and adjust to meet the unique circumstances of a particular morning or child or subject matter. This improvisation fine-tunes their actions to better and more responsibly serve their students; like musical improvisation, it is neither capricious nor random. And in this improvisation, dynamic teachers reveal the textured harmonics of their philosophy of professional commitment.

How does this philosophy play out in the classroom? How do dynamic teachers fashion caring learning environments for students? How do they facilitate student learning? These are the fundamental questions of practice described in the next chapter.

Note

1. We are indebted to Dorys Popovich-Brennan for suggesting Vivaldi's *Four Seasons* as the basis for the graphic presented in Figure 4.1.

5

The Facilitator

Enacting an Inquiring Classroom

Dynamic teachers facilitate classroom learning. What does "facilitate learning" mean? What kind of learning environments do dynamic teachers create? How do they use questioning to help students learn? How do they coordinate the learning process? Maggie and Don shape safe environments where children can explore, interact, and learn.

Maggie pushed open the door to the common area with her shoulder. Her arms were overflowing with the materials she had collected. The area was really beginning to resemble a town. More and more children were having success at finding the building materials they needed to represent their store in the town. The sun poured through the windows on the east side of the room, and Maggie felt good. She was always mildly amazed that, even after 11 years, she still got excited as a unit took shape.

"No year is ever the same," she thought. "The kids are always different, and each time they generate different questions. I've always had classes study the westward movement, but this group wanted to know about stores and towns." Maggie thought back to the day she and Don had introduced the study of the west. They began by asking the children what they knew about people who moved. Many of the children had recently moved themselves or knew relatives who had moved, so they offered a range of ideas, from reasons why to emotions they felt. Then Maggie asked if any of the reasons or emotions they had identified might be true for people who moved west as the United States developed. Carlos nearly jumped out of his seat.

"My uncles came up to the city from the islands to find work. How could that have happened back then? There were no cities!"

"Don't we all live near the city because of our parents' jobs—just like Carlos's uncles? That's because jobs are in cities now. Maybe it was jobs that people went out west looking for— maybe not to towns or cities," suggested Michael.

"I think some people then did live in towns, didn't they? I've seen them on TV shows about the frontier. They were just different," was Nancy's contribution.

The children continued to offer ideas and ask questions, revealing scattered knowledge and some misconceptions.

"Did people buy things? Or did they make everything?"

"I read about one-room schoolhouses. Weren't they in towns?"

"What if you needed a doctor? A hospital?"

"They didn't have movies or videos or TV. What did they do for fun?"

"I want to know if there were grocery stores."

Don had asked, "When do people need a grocery store?"

"Maybe some farmers started to have extra and wanted to sell it," suggested Bobbie.

"Yeah, and the doctor and the . . . maybe the barber needed to buy feed because he didn't farm," added Amid.

"Why would people need a barber? Couldn't they cut their own hair?" asked Don.

The questions flowed back and forth. Then Lindy asked if any malls existed in the old west. "What is a mall? I mean, how would you describe a mall? What are characteristics of a mall?" probed Maggie.

Lindy replied, "You know how a mall is a bunch of stores under one roof? Were there any of those?"

"Can you think of anything that would be like a mall in your idea of a western town? We'll need to explore this one," said Don.

They had continued to generate questions until they formed the idea of building a western town. Maggie and Don guided the group to choose a time period and place for their town. They zeroed in on the 1880s in the Great Plains.

A shuffling at the doorway broke into Maggie's thoughts. Don entered and handed her a cup. "I stopped by for some coffee for us. You're here early! So . . . what have we here?"

"I'm working on one of the shops. By the way," Maggie groaned, "Randy's mom called again. This time, she complained that we are not teaching because we're asking the kids to construct their own village. I satisfied her for the moment. I wish she'd talk to Randy. He's such an articulate kid. If she'd only consider that he has valid ideas, she could see how much he knows. Then maybe she wouldn't always be so critical."

Sonia arrived. "You two are always telling me to reflect on what I do. That's not easy. Look at that wallpaper Martha's group designed for the hotel. I cannot for the life of me figure out how I taught Martha's group about patterns and angles fitting together. There's no hope for me!"

"Maybe you didn't teach them; they taught themselves. You didn't have to give them a formal lesson on tessellating shapes on a plane. You gave them the tiles and the protractor and the box. What exactly did they learn? How did they show you?" asked Maggie. "I know I'm a pain about this, but I have to be able to describe what they know and how I know they know!"

"Okay! Okay! I'm working on it. Meanwhile, I know that I could never have been a seamstress in the west. How do I tell the kids that I made dresses mostly for shady ladies?" asked Sonia.

Don laughed. "Let them figure it out themselves. Those who do will be able to handle the concept."

Children began entering the room. Several carried materials. They began working at their places as Maggie, Don, and Sonia moved among them.

Amid carried a brown jacket and a Bible. "This wasn't easy for me, Ms. Clark. The towns only had a church—there was only one religion—Protestant with a minister. And they didn't wear any special robes or anything. Just a plain jacket. And I had to borrow a Bible."

"What if you were not Protestant? What if you were Jewish?" asked Maggie.

"All I read about was the one minister. I don't know," answered Amid.

"Amid's wrong. Some towns had big cathedrals. There were a lot of Catholics. I know. I saw a cathedral when my family went on vacation," interrupted Nancy.

"Where I used to live, they had an old mission. When people first went there, everyone worked for the church. My grandma said that they all came because of the church," Rosita told everyone.

"Do you think all towns in the west were the same? Maybe some had ministers and others had priests? How can we find out?" probed Maggie.

"The story I read told about a traveling minister," added Kaaba.

"Did people of one religion sometimes settle together?" Maggie suggested.

"I heard about a group call the Mormons. They all went to a place in the desert together," said Joel.

"Why would people have settled the desert? That's stupid! How could they live there?" scoffed Billy.

"Why do you think people would have settled in a desert?" asked Maggie.

"Maybe they were trying to get away from people who made fun of them," suggested Lydia.

Maggie pulled a group together. "We've got a lot of questions here about religion on the frontier. Let's list them and then decide how we can find information to start to answer them." The children gathered around an easel and tossed out questions. Next they suggested sources of information, and they discussed how they could know if the source was telling the truth.

Another group had gathered around Don. They were exploring ways to decide how much space each person got in the town. Don's questions helped them relate the size of their "lots" in the class to those a local merchant might have in a frontier town. Sonia cut pieces of heavy string for the students, who began to measure the lots. "How much will each foot be worth?" asked Don. "How will you decide?"

During recess, Maggie, Don, and Sonia huddled to review the morning session and consider any revisions for the before-lunch time, when the children would be writing. Sonia expressed some skepticism. "I still can't get over the way we don't separate the reading and math and other subjects. Lyle seemed confused that we were mixing math and social studies when we began to measure the size of the lots to scale. He thought it meant their buildings were really smaller!"

Don agreed. "You're right. Lyle didn't get it. Kids can think of 'scaling down' in a lot of ways, but his interpretation is way off base. At least we know that that's the way he is thinking! So . . . we'll work with him until he builds some sort of common understanding."

"One thing is for sure—the children in this class are certainly not afraid to share their interpretations—whatever they may be!" laughed Sonia.

*   *   *   *   *

Maggie's and Don's classroom is lively, with children offering their views and asking questions. Answers are not tightly connected to questions, and questions lead to more questions. Lessons are not arranged in a clear and prescribed order; rather, experiences and information emerge from the children and teachers themselves. All contributions are accepted and probed. Together, students grapple with ideas to make sense of the experience or information. Yet purposes are evident, and knowledge does take shape. Expectations are high, and results are demanded. Children find the classroom a safe place to explore and test their ideas against what is already known and what others are developing.

The teacher's role in this setting is complex and challenging. Not simple knowledge transmission, it goes beyond traditional instruction. Dynamic teachers create, facilitate, question, connect, and coordinate. They create an environment that is safe and rich with opportunities for children to make meaning. They facilitate understanding by providing means and authority for children to interact. They question children to engage them deeply in the search for knowledge. They connect children's constructions with each other's and with existing social constructions. And they coordinate the interactions that take place in this learning environment—those between children, between children and materials, between children and information or ideas, and between children and external resources. Dynamic teachers are facilitators of learning.

What does it mean to be a facilitator? What does a facilitator do? The word "facilitate" comes from the Latin word meaning "to make easy." But we have found that the work in dynamic teachers' classrooms is not easy. These classrooms, however, are places where it is easy for children to work hard. Dynamic teachers facilitate by enabling students' learning; that is, they provide the means and authority for students to take responsibility for their own learning. They also construct environments where multiple paths can be explored, leading through, around, and within what the student is trying to learn. The tasks of this role may seem overwhelming, but dynamic teachers know themselves and what they stand for, and they are confident in their knowledge of the subjects they teach. Thus they create environments where children can easily explore existing knowledge, probe deeply and test their own understandings, and build shared constructs. This chapter examines the many dimensions of the dynamic teacher's role as facilitator of learning within the classroom.

Creating

Maggie's and Don's first priority is establishing a safe but challenging world within their classroom. Their aim is to create the conditions that enable children to interpret and understand phenomena for themselves, to develop new schema that enable them to live better in their worlds. The primary condition is safety. Children need to feel safe, both physically and emotionally, to be able to take the risks required for meaningful learning. Maggie and Don know that many of their children live in dangerous and threatening worlds: Sonny has seen his brother shot by a gang member; Allie faces sporadic beatings at home; for years, Richard has worked his way around drug dealers on his way home. All children face, at some time, to some degree, in some form, pressure or ridicule from other students. Children learn to cope with adversity, but Maggie and Don do not want their classroom to add to the adversity in any student's life.

Maggie and Don ensure safety by establishing clear and reasonable, but high, expectations. Children in class know the rules: You cannot hurt yourself or others; you cannot break a law; you must respect other people's reasonable requests; your work must be the best you can do (Bucci & Rallis, 1979). Consequences are known and accepted. Quality standards are mutually established by the teacher and all the learners and are publicly displayed. This degree of structure allows children the freedom to question and explore.

A closely related condition for exploration and questioning is the enhancement of individual self-esteem. Maggie's and Don's respect for each other's and their students' individual abilities is obvious. They defer to one another's expertise. They recognize that students do not arrive as empty vessels; rather, Maggie and Don seek to uncover each child's story. They openly appreciate the different experiences and perspectives students offer. Their questions are genuine; they do not settle for superficial answers. Their modeling of their own values sets a compelling tone for the students. Students not only grow to believe in their own capabilities, they also grow confident enough to seek help from each other.

Another condition for exploration and questioning is the opportunity for active experience. Dewey, Piaget, Vygotsky—all maintain that children build knowledge through interaction. Maggie and Don create an environment rich with opportunities for children to interact—with ideas, with people, with objects, with each other. They believe that to know something, the learner must act on it and make it part of himself or herself. Children must move, dissect, correct, combine, take apart, and put together things so that they may understand them. Thus Maggie's and Don's classroom is full—with books, puzzles, pictures, animals, words, plants, talk, people.

Because they know that as children learn they invent and construct their world anew, Maggie and Don expect their room to change by the end of each day. Whether the process is occurring inside each child's head or in observable actions, the transformation occurs. Maggie and Don want an environment where children can test and share their constructions of the world. This year the children have chosen to transform explicitly the objects in the room to make a frontier town. In doing so, they interact with each other. Each student brings different knowledge, different perspectives to the classroom. Maggie and Don see the children's diversity itself as a resource. The diverse ideas stimulate deeper and richer constructions.

Finally, children need time—time to learn at their own pace, to interact, and to test their new inventions. At the beginning, they need time to feel safe enough to risk a leap into new activities and new thoughts. They need time to share ideas with others. And they need time to reflect on and to revise their new discoveries. Some activities may last longer than planned; others may be brief. Some children may fly through an activity, whereas others may stay with the same activity forever. Maggie and Don realize that a totally teacher-directed class will not allow this time. So they must also build in time for children to take responsibility to plan and organize their own time. The environment they create must allow time to be flexible, not rigidly allocated.

Having created a safe, respectful, interactive environment with flexible time, Maggie and Don can focus on what is most important—the children's inquiry.

Questioning

As children interact, they build knowledge. The knowledge-building process is easier if someone responds to students' questions and pushes their questions farther along new pathways. The response is not to answer the question but to validate its importance. The validation gives the child authority to continue the search for knowledge. The questioning demands that the learner interact profoundly with the experience. Thus a dynamic teacher facilitates students' learning through questioning.

Maggie and Don begin with their students' questions. Students' own questions reveal best what they care about most. Although Maggie and Don have goals for the knowledge and skill they want their students to acquire, they trust that they can reach these goals through students' interests. As one of the dynamic teachers said, "Our town's fourth-grade curriculum says we must cover simple machinery and rocks and minerals. I trust I can start anywhere and get to rocks and minerals and simple machinery."

Beane's (1990) work in middle schools reveals that the key to unlocking students' motivation is their own questions. He stresses that learners must be interested and motivated to engage with ideas and construct meaning. If children are not constructing, they are accepting. Accepting is not learning.

By acknowledging and using student questions, dynamic teachers say, "Your thoughts are important and worthwhile. The knowledge you are seeking is real. I value what you have to offer." They open possibilities for connecting the child's questions with questions other people are asking. Most important, the dynamic teacher supports the child's process of learning how to learn. In a teacher-directed classroom, children are not encouraged to believe that they can initiate the learning process; only "adult" questions seem valid. In the dynamic teacher's classroom, the children see that they have control, and thus responsibility, over what they learn. They learn to value each other's questions and thinking, as well as their teacher's.

Teachers' questions are also important in Maggie's and Don's classroom. Teachers' questions have several purposes. They aim to push new interpretations and deeper understandings, to suggest new perspectives—to yield new inventions. Duckworth (1987) suggests the kinds of questions that help this process: "What do you mean? How did you do that? Why do you say that? How does that fit in with what she just said? Could you give me an example? How did you figure that?" (p. 96). In sum, the questions encourage critical thinking.

Not any question will do, however. Maggie and Don seldom ask questions for which they already have an answer. They are genuinely interested in hearing where the student will take the question. They ask authentic questions—ones that both the teacher and the student want to pursue. The questions push the children to think deeper in their own terms and to articulate thoughts in their own words. After several girls in class read *Caddie Woodlawn*, they questioned whether some of Caddie's behavior was realistic. Don asked, "What in the story makes you doubt Caddie? When did you first realize that the author may have exaggerated? Although you may never have felt you could save a whole town, have you ever felt that you could and should change a situation? What did you do? How did it affect others? How might you have written Caddie's story differently?"

In other instances, Don's or Maggie's questions may be geared to spur experimentation: "Do you think it will work? Why don't you try it out?" These questions encourage the child to test the viability of his or her invention. When a small group in the class proposed a method of goods-for-services exchange in place of money for the town, Maggie and Don teachers encouraged them to test the plan with the class. Until they actually used the method in class, they could only hypothesize its merits and pitfalls. The questions that grew out of its use enabled them to improve the plan.

Dynamic teachers, then, use authentic questioning to enhance the quality of the knowledge children are building. The teachers also use questions to connect these constructions with those of others.

Connecting the Constructs

Learning is more than the process of active individual construction; it also involves a process of enculturating the learner into the existing community of knowledge and practices of society (Cobb, 1994, p. 13). The teacher's role is to build bridges between the experiences of the child and the knowledge of experts (Ball, 1993):

> *How* do I create experiences for my students that connect with what they now know and care about but that also transcend the present? *How* do I value their interests and also connect them to ideas and traditions growing out of centuries of mathematical exploration and invention? (p. 375, emphasis in original)

Communities of knowledge exist. They are continually growing, and today's students can contribute to the future shape of the bodies of knowledge in these communities. The dynamic teacher asks, How can the classroom simulate real communities so that students may master the norms and practices of those communities? (Driver et al., 1994). The adopt-a-shop idea is one of Maggie's and Don's attempts to connect their class with real communities. What would it take to survive as a baker? A grocer? A shoemaker? The frontier town simulation opens possibilities for children to interact with real communities of knowledge: history, sociology, mathematics, art, and more.

All children make sense of their world in their own ways, and the teacher is obligated to help his or her students make sense of certain material. But the child's sense making or constructs must be shared with others to test their viability as community knowledge (see von Glasersfeld, 1992, p. 381). Knowledge that is meaningful within a culture is socially constructed, validated, and communicated. What counts as a problem and what counts as a solution are highly normative (Solomon, 1989). Children are asked to do more than problem solve for themselves. They need to try out, to test their constructs to see if they can be understood and shared.

Dynamic teachers ask children to explain their understandings to classmates. Children need to articulate the problem and to explain it to others. The task for children in a dynamic teacher's classroom is both to understand and to understand how others understand. Making sense of the concept of scale will not be enough for Lyle. He will also have to use his understanding with his classmates. In doing so, he will have to negotiate among other children's understandings. For some students, this process of social construction out of individual constructs is easy. For Lyle, who is having enough trouble just "getting it" for himself, the process may be difficult—or he may find that the process can be assisted by others. Don and Maggie and Sonia seek to understand his learning process and to connect him with his peers.

The teacher's role as mediator is important in negotiating the discourse that connects individuals with the community and connects new ideas with cultural standards. Teachers, as professionals, have access to the culturally accepted symbolic world that they are obligated to bring to their students. Dynamic teachers do not impose existing symbolic interpretations on students. Rather, they offer opportunities for children to make sense of the social constructions. For example, Maggie's and Don's students learned what historians say was accepted as religion on the frontier and contrasted that with what they determine is accepted today. Also, the children considered why laws we have today may not have worked a century ago and vice versa. Children connect with this knowledge through defining, examining and exploring, and reflecting upon it. Their connection with an existing construct yields a new construct.

A fourth-grade class studying the pilgrims provides an illustration of connections yielding new understanding. The students asked how the pilgrims treated property: Did individual families own their goods privately? What about land? Did they share food? Their teacher offered ideas on community ownership, telling students about various communes that have existed in American history. The students decided they would try community ownership of pencils and reading books. They could take these items from a common source and return them when they were no longer using them or at the end of the day. Shortly, the pencil supply was depleted and several books were misplaced. The group considered various rules, and the teacher referred them to the way libraries operate. As a group, the children then built a structure and process for their community to share materials. Their construct was a result of the integration of their individual understandings and existing social understandings. A new construct resulted.

Coordinating

A classroom in which students build their own understandings, test them out and explain them to classmates, and connect them with others and with existing knowledge is a busy place. Students could easily get lost, fall through the cracks, become confused, develop unworkable interpretations. A final role of the teacher as facilitator is to coordinate the tasks in the classroom so that children build meaningful and essential knowledge of quality. The dynamic teacher works to ensure that all parts work together and that shared understandings are developed.

The dynamic teacher is faced with two levels of coordination. First, he or she must help the individual child coordinate his or her internal process of equilibration and disequilibration (Piaget, 1970b). Children create new, more complex schemes by modifying older, simpler ones. The teacher sees that children do not settle for a comfortable stasis by coordinating the questions and information that push the learners and upset their equilibrium. The teacher also coordinates time and activities so that the learner's dissonance is resolved with new constructs. We see Maggie responding to the children's ideas about religion by organizing their questions and their search for information.

The teacher must also coordinate across children. Each child brings his or her own special worldview drawn from his or her own family and experience, innate abilities and talents, and present developmental level. These differences offer rich material to support cognitive development. They create the zones of proximal development that Vygotsky (1978) says awaken internal processes essential for learning. The teacher sees that children of different perspectives and abilities and developmental levels have safe opportunities to work together on tasks that are meaningful to them.

A dynamic teacher asks children to draw their image of the ideal classroom. A plethora of ideas are suggested, and all are accepted. Then the teacher asks the class to come up with one design that all can agree would be ideal. First, the class must decide how it will decide. After intense negotiation, the children agree upon a plan. As a result, a design emerges that draws from many images and suggestions.

Coordination may occur through modeling. The children watch Maggie and Don interact with each other and Sonia and with other faculty. They watch Maggie and Don interact with students. The teachers' interactions set a tone the students can emulate. When Billy scoffs at Joel's information about settling the desert, Maggie counters with a question that enables another student to suggest an interpretation. Maggie watches and responds to children's behavior. In turn, Maggie's behavior provides the stimulus for the children's behavior. Children become comfortable questioning and probing each other.

In a classroom where children are encouraged to build their own complex knowledge, coordination becomes even more important to develop shared common knowledge. Children need to work together to test their understandings with others. Dynamic teachers encourage and support children's communication. They discuss, they present, they demonstrate. These teachers emphasize products as much as process. The frontier town is a visible, tangible product as well as an engaging process. A group of students interested in law and law enforcement chose certain questions to explore in their research and discuss together, comparing and contrasting what they understand about laws and compliance in the old west to lawmakers, police, and courts, as they know them today. The products they create together may range from a code of laws for their town to a mock trial they enact. To create the products, they must first test their constructions on one another. The teachers coordinate the activities around the conversations and the products.

Effective coordination is especially important today to ensure that children learn how to learn. Materials abound; information from a multitude of sources is plentiful. Children do not need to memorize much, but they do need to access information. They need to know what they are looking for, where to go for it, how to interpret its value to them. Dynamic teachers expose their students to the multiplicity of resources available to them in their community, whatever their economic status. A dynamic teacher in a struggling urban setting brought in local merchants, as did Maggie and Don; one used a local artist; another found a nearby agency whose computers with CD-ROMs are available to students. Yet another asked parents to share real-life problems they encountered on their jobs; the students offered solutions. Dynamic teachers coordinate all kinds of resources (including parents and other community people, as we will see in Chapter 7) to the benefit of the students' learning.

SUMMARY

Dynamic teachers facilitate the learning in their classroom by making it easy for students to work productively and to be excited about their work. A third grader said about his dynamic teacher, "She's not a 'hard' teacher, but she sure makes us work hard!" These are teachers who create the conditions in which children feel safe to experiment and explore, and where they have the time to make mistakes and try again. These are teachers who question so that students will push deeper into their own understandings, and who will connect them with the learnings of others and existing interpretations of knowledge. They coordinate all the activity in the classroom so that neither learning nor students fall through any cracks. In the next chapter, we take a look at how dynamic teachers assess and evaluate what students have learned in their classes.

The Inquirer

Asking Critical Questions

Dynamic teachers use assessment strategies to support students' inquiry, to evaluate students' learning, to help students evaluate their own learning, and to report about learning to important constituents. Maggie and Don ask, What have we agreed is important for students to know and be able to do? What are students actually doing in the classroom? How can I know what they are learning? How can I ethically report this learning to parents, administrators, and other legitimate audiences?

Grade report time was approaching at the O'Henry School, so Maggie and Don were reviewing work with each student. Everyone had a folder to keep samples of work or products or to refer to something they had accomplished. The folders included a variety of "products": writing samples, tests, artwork, charts and graphs, problem solutions, descriptions or reports of an activity, journal entries. A few students had copies of a video a parent had made of the frontier town being constructed.

One activity all students had been asked to do was write a job description for a position at the store or business they had adopted in their frontier town, Sweetwater. They were to post the description, and other students who were interested could apply. The children had also been asked to compare the jobs of old with current jobs in the corresponding stores they had adopted in the town near school. Maggie looked for this comparison in Billy's folder. She didn't find it. She also realized he had not posted a description.

"Aw, Ms. Clark, why do I have to write up a job description for the general store clerk in Sweetwater? Everybody knows what a store clerk does. It's boring," complained Billy.

"So now nobody has applied for the job. Somebody might have been interested in being a clerk. What does a clerk do? Describe it, Billy," urged Maggie.

"They just ring up the prices on things people buy and take their money or credit cards," answered Billy.

"Maybe that's what happens today in town. But what about in Sweetwater—100 years ago? Did stores have cash registers? Credit cards?"

"How am I supposed to know? I thought we were just supposed to find out what the merchant we adopted does. I didn't think about a store clerk's job changing. I'd guess it was just as boring a hundred years ago," said Billy.

"Why did you choose to adopt the grocery store?"

"My brother clerks there. But he doesn't like it."

"Still, a grocery store is pretty necessary today, I think. Hmmm, I wonder if you lived in Sweetwater a long time ago, would your brother have worked in the grocery store? Would his responsibilities have been the same? Would there even have been a grocery store? Do you think you learned enough to be able to compare now with then? What do you think about what you learned? Did you answer any of your questions about the job with new information?" asked Maggie. When Billy agreed that he had not found any new information, Maggie suggested they make a plan for him to follow.

Maggie thought about how working with Billy could be discouraging. She found that he needed more direction—and motivation—than most of the children. She commented to Don at lunch, "Billy always reminds me how hard teaching is. Just when I think I've made a point, explained something well, I realize that Billy doesn't get it."

"I'm really glad you were reviewing his work today. Otherwise, we might have just gone on thinking that everyone understood what we were trying to do. It's a little scary to think that Billy—maybe others—missed the point about jobs," noted Don.

"Fortunately, I looked at Joel's folder after Billy's. Of course, Joel is at the other end of the spectrum. I mean, he's already decided what he's mastered and what he needs more work on. He asked for help on figuring out sale prices with percents off! He told me he realized he did not understand that when he tried to explain it to Marcie," Maggie reported.

"At least you give him that chance. And Billy, too. All I can remember about assessment from school is tests and tests," moaned Sonia. "And if we didn't do well, it was our fault. A lot of times when I got a bad grade I just did not have a clue about what was expected."

"I kind of like tests. As long as I don't expect or force a bell curve. Tests really let me know what the kids have learned. And sometimes I can see that I haven't really taught it. Remember the time I was doing graphs, and I never explained what I meant by the 'axis'? Some of the class figured it out by themselves, but most thought I was talking about chopping wood!" Don laughed.

"But let's get back to Billy. . . . How do we get children like him to take some responsibility for their own learning?" wondered Maggie. "I worked out a plan with him —what are his questions; where can he find information; what should he do with the information. I will have to monitor him to see what he does with it."

"What's missing is a way he can monitor his own progress," said Don. "Maybe we can ask him to decide if he wants to be the Sweetwater store clerk. If not, then he has to do a 'Tom Sawyer'—talk someone else into doing it. Something like that—so that he can judge his success himself."

"I think it's especially important for Billy to judge his own success because his mom and stepdad aren't much help. Billy told me they probably won't come in for the conference. I've been wondering how you get so many parents' support using different assessments. I've heard a lot of teachers say that parents still want traditional grades and standardized tests," said Sonia.

"It didn't happen overnight! Parents worked with us; they told us what would count as learning for them. Maggie and I clearly value process—how Johnny gets the answer—as much as the answer. But parents want products. So you see how we ensure products—the children do things. The doing often involves explaining how they created a product."

"I guess parents believe we know where we are going. Columbus is a good analogy," suggested Maggie. "I doubt he would have gotten any support at all if he'd really been heading for the unknown. Isabella and Ferdinand had an image of the Indies. Like Columbus, we offer an acceptable image of what we expect the children to learn."

"And, like Columbus we often end up in a different place. But I hope we are a whole lot better assessing where the class does get than Columbus was!" concluded Don as they rejoined their students.

*   *   *   *   *

Dynamic teachers such as Maggie and Don are rethinking the roles and purposes of the assessment and evaluation of student learning; they question the basic premises behind standard assessment measures; they look back at the untold narrowness and damage of traditional ways of evaluating student learning. They search for a new synthesis that is integral to teaching and learning and has at its center the academic, social, and personal growth of each individual child. This synthesis is captured by the metaphors of portraits or videos, where the central purpose is to build an archive of student learning over time, and stands in stark contrast to the traditional, deficit models of assessment. In inquiry-oriented, learner-centered classrooms, dynamic teachers provide strategies for helping students assess their personal archives: to review them periodically, to review what they have learned and how they have grown, and to evaluate critically what they need to learn. These teachers envision assessment as a crucial element in taking each student's learning forward to more complex levels. This assessment, moreover, takes place within an agreed-upon set of standards of what students should know and be able to do to function successfully, ethically, and productively in society.

Maggie and Don are creating an evaluation-minded classroom. For them, assessment is the process of amassing evidence of learning sufficient to evaluate that learning ethically. They understand that they cannot directly assess learning because it is an internal process, but they can assess evidence that learning has taken place. They agree that "learning cannot actually be seen because the processes that go on in a learner's mind take many forms, are specific to the learner, and are not fully understood by the learner himself" (Mirman Owen, Cox, & Watkins, 1994, p. 44). Thus gathering evidence precedes judgments about learning. With such evidence, evaluations of a student's growth (changes) and progress (in relation to an agreed-upon set of standards) can be made by the learner, his or her peers, the teacher, and other interested parties such as parents and families (Mirman Owen, Cox, & Watkins, 1994, p. 44).

In an evaluation-minded classroom, students take responsibility for learning and teachers take responsibility for teaching, but these demarcations often blur. Students also assume some responsibility for the learning of their peers, often acting as teachers, and teachers hold themselves responsible for furthering their own growth and development, clearly modeling the role of learner. Accountability is not hierarchical, with children accountable only to teachers and teachers accountable only to an external bureaucratic power such as state testing, "the curriculum," or the central office. Rather, accountability is horizontal (Rivzi, 1990), with each individual accountable to and responsible for the classroom community. As described in Chapter 4, such accountability is integral to dynamic teachers' philosophy of professional commitment.

In a classroom with horizontal accountability, students primarily answer to themselves and to each other; teachers answer primarily to students and to each other. Because of the community and societal contexts in which schools are embedded, however, teachers are also accountable for student learning to larger audiences—a form of vertical accountability. First and foremost of these audiences are parents and families. But the extent to which parents want and are able to participate in the conversation about learning varies enormously. Thus, to the extent to which parents are an identified part of the community, they share in the accountability. Dynamic teachers, moreover, strive to involve parents and families more fully in that conversation, building a community that supports learning at home and in school. With an emphasis on horizontal accountability in the classroom, however, an ethic of inquiry is created by recognizing everyone's responsibility for the success of all community members and by providing opportunities for reflection. Accountability for the total community's learning is shared.

In this chapter we explore how authentic assessment is becoming integral to teaching and learning in learner-centered classrooms where inquiry is honored. We contrast traditional views of evaluating student learning with views of dynamic teachers. We consider how dynamic teachers articulate what they expect students to learn, what they do to facilitate that learning, how they look at what students are doing, and how they can know what their students have learned. We also focus on the strategies that dynamic teachers share with students to support and challenge them as they learn to assess their own work.

Rethinking the
Assessment of Student Learning

Dynamic teachers eschew the assumptions of traditional assessment as inconsistent with their philosophies of teaching and learning. Because dynamic teachers do not simply transmit existing knowledge, they ask how they can use traditional assessment practices. Assessment of the exploring, seeking, and explaining that occurs in their classrooms requires more than a fill-in-the-blank test. Assessing the learning of each diverse individual learner in the classroom can seem overwhelming when each student is studying and learning different things at a different pace! Often students are working in a group—how can the teacher possibly sort out what each child is doing and learning? Assessing complex problem-solving is much more formidable than testing students' memory of the state capitols.

How can a teacher possibly find the time to observe all the work and interactions of every child in the classroom? How can he or she find the time to strategize with each student to decide all the pieces of work that need to go into that child's portfolio?

The answer is to honor some of the old practices while creating new ones for assessing student learning based on a clear understanding of learning and its purposes, coupled with a vision that responsibility for learning is shared. Together with their students, dynamic teachers create evidentiary archives or portfolios that assess learning in a variety of ways ("multimethod") and that capture the diversity of the products of that learning ("multitrait"). These archives also gather evidence of student learning over time, rather than at some arbitrary end point. With assessments gathered through both traditional and authentic methods that capture the complexity of student learning over time, a more full and rich portrait of learning is possible than when one relies on a single method. These assessments then become the evidence upon which judgments about student growth and progress can be made.

Committing to comprehensive assessment, however, takes a sometimes agonizing appraisal of current practice and demands courage and commitment on the part of teachers. Pressures come from varied and articulate parties to continue in the past tradition. Teachers learned the old methods through their own experiences in schools as students, through their teacher preparation experiences, and from their veteran colleagues. New practices, designed for authentic learning and assessment, require a dramatic shift in focus toward the learner and how the learner constructs knowledge, acquires skills, and thinks about his or her learning, as well as toward the opportunities the teacher provides for learning.

Teachers like Maggie and Don use multiple methods and products of assessment to create inquiry-oriented classrooms. They use assessment to help children examine their own work and progress, reflect on what they are learning, and become more aware of their own strengths and areas they need to develop. Dynamic teachers want assessment to help children become self-directed, to want to learn and improve their skills, and to believe that they can. They want assessment to help children gain confidence and fine-tune ways of learning that work best for them. They want assessment to encourage and help children learn how to make the most of working with other people.

Maggie and Don firmly believe that assessment should enable the student to evaluate himself or herself and, thus, to function better with others in life and work. They also acknowledge the importance of public assessment, enabling the community to judge the progress and growth of students' mastery of essential knowledge and skills. Dynamic teachers, then, are trying to alter assessment to bring it closer to current theory about learning and to ground it in ethical conceptions of practice.

Inquiring About Student Learning

Images

Maggie and Don have a vision of what their students should know and be able to do that is framed by a set of standards (Marzano, 1992). These standards are grounded in what the community believes about student learning, which in turn is shaped by larger regional, national, and international conceptions of what constitutes an educated person. But Maggie's and Don's standards are not limiting, nor are they universal or "standard standards." Their standards require students to pursue world-class "nonstandardized standards" (Schwarz, 1994). Standards cannot

> provide a simplistic "single form" alternative to simplistic units or tests. We must have a locally initiated, locally controlled system of standards setting that is at once knowledgeable of the national and international state of the art of schooling and that respects, celebrates, and harbors the highest expectations for all of an area's own local children. (p. 34)

To determine these "world-class" standards, Maggie and Don use their professional knowledge in conjunction with community members' ideas to decide what their students should learn. They draw from the standards set by professional associations (such as those set by the National Council of Teachers of Mathematics) or those accompanying research-based instructional programs such as Dimensions of Learning (see Marzano et al., 1993). Whenever possible, they work with task forces in their school and community to solicit input and garner support. They write goals both broad ("understands how basic geometric shapes are used in the planning of communities") and specific ("accurately converts U.S. distance measurements into metric distance measurements"). They offer clear, but not confining, images of what they expect: For instance, they point to stories children like to read (*Caddie Woodlawn*; *My Side of the Mountain*) as examples of "good writing." Like Columbus, they offer a compelling vision of what is possible.

Dynamic teachers also engage students in developing indicators of quality. They understand that "the more students help design assessments and assess their own learning, the more they will understand assessment procedures, learn from assessment activities, and internalize high standards" (Mirman Owen, Cox, & Watkins, 1994, p. 46). Thus, they ask students, What makes a good story? What must an experiment include to be able to test a hypothesis? What goes into a winning debate? If students are to judge their own work, they must understand and construct the tools for assessment. Students themselves help set meaningful standards. Together, students and teachers conjure images upon which they can act and assess. A dynamic teacher describes how her students are becoming able to articulate goals for their learning and assess their progress toward those goals: "They don't always come running up to me to ask what I think. More and more, they can tell me what *they* think is good about their work."

The Process

With this vision of learning based on agreed-upon standards, the next step is teaching. We have defined the dynamic teacher's teaching as facilitating. As facilitators, dynamic teachers are responsible for initiating the process, and they are indirectly responsible for products. During this stage, the teacher asks, What am I actually teaching? Are my purposes evident? What do the students see, hear, and feel during the experience? What are the students making of the experience? What are the students actually doing with the experience?

The students are responsible for engaging in the process. They ask, What are the purposes of this experience? What am I expected to do? What does it mean to me? What can I do with it? How do I interact with others about it?

This stage requires action. A particular lesson or experience can act out or test the teacher's mental constructions and the students' manipulation of or reconstruction of them. As the teacher and students act and interact, the teacher looks at where the students are going, at what they are doing. The process is both action and inquiry because both the teacher and the students actively construct knowledge about the experience as they interact with it and with each other.

Fullan (1993) describes the process of educational change as "ready, fire, aim"; these descriptors can also apply to learner-centered teaching. Fullan alters the expected sequence to reveal that until the teacher "fires" and the students "fire" in response, the true "aim" is not visible. "As people talk, try things out, inquire, retry—all of this jointly—people become more skilled, ideas become clearer, shared commitment gets stronger" (p. 31). The action of firing gives teachers and students the substance for their reflection and inquiry, which in turn leads to revised plans and actions.

Process in dynamic teachers' classrooms emphasizes conversations in which students explain their new and emerging understandings with other students and with the teacher. Conversations allow opportunities for students to test their constructions: Does it make sense to others? Does it work? Can others use it? How can it be improved? Can it be combined with others? Can it contribute to a shared understanding? Recall Maggie telling Don about Joel, who felt that, "I'm never really sure I am right about something until I explain it to someone else."

Reflection, by both the teacher and students, plays a major role in the process stage. Dynamic teachers assess their actions by reflecting on them. They are aware of the possibility of "misfires." Their facilitation may have unintended consequences, either positive or negative. A concept they intended to convey or activity they intended the students to experience may not have happened at all or may have produced unexpected responses. They know they need to consider what happened and the effect. If, for example, children are expected to perform based on information they were not provided, or essential directions were missed, the teacher must rethink his or her evaluation or refacilitate the experience. Reflection assists the teacher to assess and be responsible for his or her teaching.

At some point in their reflection, students will use the rubrics, either formal or informal, that have been developed for the specific tasks and situations in which they are engaged. Because rubrics describe levels of performance, they can provide important information about what students know and can do. The agreed-upon standards for performance provide a basis for conversations in which both teacher and students can assess student progress. By contributing to the reflection process, rubrics promote learning.

This stage furthers inquiry into student learning; it includes action and reflection and action, construction, interaction, reconstruction. Assessment at this stage focuses on amassing appropriate evidence of learning; evaluation is tentative and interim, or informative and formative. During this stage, students and teachers use assessment data to inform them about where the student is: What knowledge or skills has he or she acquired? How can he or she use these to perform? They use these assessment data to make formative evaluations about what the student needs to work on and how the teacher should revise his or her teaching. The class has fired and has realigned the aim.

The Product

Part of the dynamic teacher's vision of learning includes products, or a range of products, that provide evidence of learning. Drawing on both their past experience and their own creativity, dynamic teachers envision possible outcomes of the learning experience. At the same time, they are open to students' ideas. They even encourage students to design their own product. They ask, How can we gather evidence that will show what students have learned? Then they offer students opportunities for choice and creativity.

Products serve two primary purposes. First, they are informative; that is, they provide evidence of growth and progress that students themselves, as well as teachers and others, can reflect on and evaluate. Portfolios, for example, structure a "repository of evidence" so that students can review and reflect as they move along in their schooling. Second, products serve a "summative" purpose in which a judgment about learning takes place in a more final form. Products serving this purpose may be group products, individual, or imposed by external demands such as norm-referenced testing. Teachers may have to impose some products because they are required by the district or the state, but they can help students make meaning out of external demands such as standardized testing.

Most importantly, the teacher and students ask, and parents want to know, what have the students learned? At this point, dynamic teachers focus on authentic products. The products may take many forms, ranging from oral presentations, demonstrations, final drafts of written work, videos, and artwork, to more traditional paper-and-pencil tests. What makes them authentic is the meaning they hold and convey. They are used to evaluate student growth and progress because they reveal or illustrate the student's mastery of a body of knowledge and a set of skills. In the products, learning and assessment overlap.

Of primary importance is that the product be meaningful to both the students and teachers. Steven Levy, the 1992-1993 Massachusetts Teacher of the Year and winner of The Walt Disney Company 1994 American Teacher for General Elementary award, asks his students to decide upon the product but stipulates that it must be real-world useful. "I never quite know where we will end up. Last year we studied the town's bicycle path. We produced a guide for townsfolk and other users of the path. The guide included a map, the history, rules, how it was built, what to expect along the way. We sold it to cover the costs of printing it."

The bicycle-path guide is a particularly useful product because its production by students incorporated all levels of learning. For example, using Bloom's (1964) taxonomy, the learning experience covered the tasks of locating and analyzing, as well as synthesizing and evaluating information. Most of these tasks were evident in the product itself. The bicycle-path guide could also be analyzed to reveal use of both declarative and procedural knowledge for all five dimensions of learning (Marzano et al., 1993): holding positive attitudes and perceptions about learning, acquiring and integrating knowledge, extending and refining knowledge, using knowledge meaningfully, and demonstrating productive habits of mind.

A product also communicates students' understandings clearly so that others may evaluate them. Thus the product is a public display, whether oral or written or drawn, whether displayed in a portfolio, in front of an audience, or on a wall. Those judging may use an agreed-upon set of quality indicators or rubrics. In creating their products, students aim to meet a set of defined standards, but they are not bound to or limited by the standards. Ideally, they have participated in defining those standards.

The product allows the teacher to say, "The students are able to do this much with the experiences they have had to this point. Are they able to do what I, as their facilitator, had hoped? If not, what might be some possible explanations? Are they able to do more?

What experiences could promote more growth and progress?" It also allows the students to assess whether they have accomplished what they hoped to.

The product is especially useful for parents and other legitimate audiences who are interested in student learning. An additional purpose of the product is to provide concrete grounds—the evidence—for conversation about what students are learning. If the product is authentic, it has meaning for parents and other adults as well. The conversation about the product with parents can be rich, as the child directs the parents' attention to his or her interpretations and asks parents and family members for theirs.

Uses of Assessment

The kind of assessment Maggie and Don use validates the student's views and abilities. As the student's actual work and the assessment of that work become more and more merged, the student sees value in his or her own thinking, exploring, and judgment. He or she sees value in the questions he or she asks, and assesses learning in terms of finding his or her own answers, refining and expanding them through discussion with others, and creating products that reflect his or her learning.

This whole process can be taken much further with the support of family members who come to understand and value the student's ability to articulate his or her own learning. Dynamic teachers take very seriously the purposes of assessment of student learning aimed toward developing greater parental and family support. In fact, one of the purposes of the assessment for Maggie and Don is to bring parents into the loop. Whereas in most schools student work is reported periodically in standard formats, Maggie and Don do more. They create opportunities for children and their parents to review the work together. Sometimes the opportunity is provided through parent conferences, but usually it is stimulated through a letter accompanying a product or group of products. The letter usually includes a space where the child asks the parent to answer specific questions about the work. In this way the child directs the parent or family member toward the specific learning he or she has been working on. Parents also see the child's efforts at self-evaluation.

Dynamic teachers recognize that self-evaluation is natural. Students want to evaluate their own work, and they enjoy the opportunity to share their evaluations with others, be they parents, peers, or their teachers. A dynamic teacher told us that

> two favorite forms of self-evaluation are emerging in my classroom. Students seem to love the "paper trail" of progress. I think that the concrete evidence of change, usually improvement, gives them the ability to write more comfortably and from a position of confidence in seeing their own actual improvement over time. This concrete change is one they can readily "see," thus more easily express in writing. They actively look for an opportunity to implement this scenario.

> Another preferred method of evaluation is to compare their own evaluations with mine or vice versa. Students listen very carefully to my explanations as to reasons for assessing their work and really try to apply those standards in their own self-evaluations. What's telling here is the perceptions of what's important to them—sometimes so close to my own thinking, at other times so different.

Dynamic teachers know that self-evaluation is a primary step toward developing skills as a lifelong learner. Students who learn to use a rubric to assess the quality of the contents of their own portfolios may, as adults, identify levels of performance to assess a sample of their products on the job. Students who identify their own quality indicators and who become comfortable using them to assess and improve their work are likely to be comfortable judging the quality of work they do as adults. Maggie and Don hope that the seamless merging of learning and assessment will stay with their students as they become reflective adults.

SUMMARY

Dynamic teachers use strategies for assessment to encourage inquiry and to promote learning. They document students' growth and progress; they gather evidence of learning; they relate this evidence to agreed-upon standards; and they share it publicly. These teachers also facilitate the development of these "habits of mind" and skills in their students, promoting their self-assessment and evaluation.

Embedded in this discussion, and at times explicit, is the notion that the community is integral to the authentic assessment of learning. While striving to include the community in defining standards for learning and appropriate, authentic assessments of that learning, dynamic teachers also build a sense of community both inside their classrooms and within the school. This dual meaning for the concept of community—having a "sense of community" and honoring the school's community—is elaborated in the next chapter.

7

The Bridger

Blurring the Boundaries Between Communities

What do dynamic teachers do to create welcoming classrooms? How do they bring the community into the classroom, and the classroom out into the community? How do they find a variety of resources to enrich their classroom? How do they define "community"? Maggie and Don offer their views of the complex nature of community, both inside and outside their classroom walls.

Maggie sagged into her chair, exhausted. It had been a very long day. Two of the three store owners she had invited had appeared at the classroom door at 10:30, just as the students were getting ready to go to art class. As hard as she and Don tried, there were always conflicts with that damnable schedule! She wished for the thousandth time that she and Don could have complete autonomy. . . . Maybe then things would go exactly as she wanted. She felt tears of frustration welling up. . . . This was no good. Trying to calm herself, she reflected on the goodwill and interest of the store owners, and the art teacher.

Tony, the art teacher, had been interested in the frontier town idea since the beginning. When he told Maggie about the class's current design project, she realized that Sonia hadn't connected with him: Sonia had thought of art period as "prep time for herself" and hadn't pursued in any detail what Tony was doing with the children. Maggie thought about her first years of teaching, when she would retreat to the teachers' room for a breather while the students went to art or gym or music. She too had not had the energy to work with those other teachers to enrich her classroom. Maggie thought about how to approach Sonia to help her draw on the resources within the school to complement and extend the curriculum. She made a mental note to talk further with Sonia about the wall-paper designs the students had created and share with her the conversation with Tony. She wanted Sonia to become more analytic about what the students were learning.

And the store owners! They were something else. . . . Zing Pao had seemed uncomfortable at first. Maggie sensed a deep cultural norm against "interfering" in the educational process. With gentle formality, however, she had eased his discomfort, encouraging him to share his experiences coming to this country and creating a marvelous small grocery store that served the community by specializing in foods from other nations. Having his child in class had helped, too. Tarik Mari, the Lebanese baker, showed the students how pita was made and shared a snack with them after art class. Patrick Reilly, the shoemaker, however, had called and left a cryptic message—something about not knowing what to do in the classroom.

Besides that, something was missing from the classroom visit of the two shopkeepers—it had seemed too much like "show and tell." What could she and Don do to make the contact between the children and these community people more fruitful? In her tired state, no ideas popped into her mind, but she was sure that putting it all "on the back burner" would help: Ideas would crop up, as they always did.

Just as the phrase "back burner" went through her mind, Maggie realized that she used that phrase a lot with the children. Katie, with all of her developmental delays, had come to rely on time and space to let her ideas emerge; using that phrase had helped her understand that her mind had its own pace, and she was beginning to know it and respect it.

Thinking of Katie brought a grin to Maggie's face. Maybe today had not been so bad!

"I'm glad someone has something to grin about," grumbled Don, interrupting Maggie's thoughts. "I was just at the special ed advisory council. Sometimes I think all they care about is their own kids and special needs." Don reported feeling frustrated at the group's seeming inability to think about what would be best for all the children. "Oh, well, if it were not for this group, I wouldn't know as much about Katie and some of our other children with special needs. Maybe their persistence pays off for us."

"At least they're interested in the academics," responded Maggie. "I talked to Howie's dad today—ran into him out on the field. He's always doing something for the school, but he doesn't care about real learning. He asks, 'Will Howie get a job? Is he safe? Is anybody else getting more breaks?' He doesn't ask, 'What is Howie learning? Is he learning to handle himself in different situations? Is he comfortable enough to think for himself?' I wish all parents could come in and work with our groups the way Sandra Wallace and Micky Nadler do. Those two belong in our classes now—and I'd say I've learned a thing or two from them."

"Whoa! I guess you're not as chipper as you looked," said Don.

"I don't know why I launched off on that old thorn. What is really worrying me is the shopkeepers." Maggie told him about her concerns and about the call from Patrick Reilly. "How can we make him comfortable enough to visit?"

"I need to pick up some photos in town today. The photo shop is next door to the shoe repair shop. Why don't I stop in and talk to him on my way home today?" Don suggested.

Later that afternoon, Don pushed open the door to the shoe repair shop and was engulfed by the warm smell of leather and polish. Patrick Reilly welcomed him with an apologetic smile. "Sorry I let you down . . . but I was too nervous. Never did well in school, you know. Liked to work with my hands—

enjoyed showing people and talking about my work, but the academic stuff—well, that wasn't my strong point."

"Why don't you talk to the kids about your work then?" suggested Don.

"Well, young folks today—they aren't interested. Never see them in the shop here."

"What got you interested in shoes? Did you know about shoemaking when you were in grade school? When did you know this was what you wanted to do?" inquired Don.

"Can't say I dreamed of being a shoemaker, now that you ask. I needed a job—times were tough for my family. My dad always got new soles on his shoes. I don't think he ever bought new shoes. So I knew old Bernie pretty well, and he let me help him. Turns out I was really good at it—and I liked doing it," Patrick reminisced.

"What kind of training did you need? How did you set up shop? What's changed in your work over the years?" Don's questions got the shoemaker talking about his work.

Finally, he brought out a book from under his work counter. "You see, Don, I love working with leather, making and repairing shoes, and would you believe that what I do now is not very much different from how shoemakers worked a hundred years ago? See, look at these pictures. . . . That's something that really amazed me . . . but kids aren't going to be interested in that, are they?"

"I guess we never told you what we have in mind," said Don, and he described what the class was doing with the frontier town and the adopt-a-shop project. "We are looking for opportunities for children to connect real-life work today with work in the frontier town. We hope they will get a sense of all the possibilities in work. Why don't we start with the children's questions?"

"I'm still nervous," protested Patrick. "But why don't I send in this tool with you. I won't tell you what it is. See what the children make of it. If they really have questions, then I'll come in."

"You've got a deal, Reilly!" The two men shook hands. "They'll have questions, all right. Who knows, maybe you'll get some kids to come in here to help you!"

Driving home, Don felt pretty satisfied with his interaction with Reilly. "Gotta remind Maggie to have faith in the community!" he thought. He remembered the warning of Diane, a fourth-grade teacher, not to bother bringing in community people—because they often let you down and didn't really understand education. "Well, Patrick Reilly will prove her wrong when he, as he put it, 'comes back to school.' "

*   *   *   *   *

The previous chapters focused on how dynamic teachers create a sense of community within their classrooms. We turn now to the larger, sometimes geographically defined, community that enriches classrooms and that students and dynamic teachers can, in turn, enrich. The fundamental questions of this chapter are, What do dynamic teachers construe as the community in that larger world that surrounds and relates to their classrooms? How do dynamic teachers manage to make a bridge to this larger world?

Defining and Relating to the Community

Dynamic teachers construe the notion of community quite broadly. One concept captures the climate, culture, and *Zeitgeist*, or spirit, of their classrooms and schools. In this sense, dynamic teachers believe that the classroom and school have a "sense of community"—a sense of caring, shared responsibility for one another and the work, and a fundamental attitude of respect. A sense of community is the tie that binds students, teachers, families, and those in the geographic community together "in special ways, to something more significant than themselves" (Sergiovanni, 1994, p. xiii).

The glue of community is relationships that shift meaning and attention from a feeling of disparate, individual *I*s to a sense of *we*. Without this sense of community, dynamic teachers believe, "school becomes a continuous uphill struggle requiring the expenditure of considerable professional energies just to stop bad things from happening" (Gregory & Smith, 1987, p. 21). Thus, working to create a sense of community is fundamental to the work of dynamic teachers and is founded in their deeply held values. It infuses their pedagogy, curriculum, approach to school organization, and leadership.

Dynamic teachers hold another conception of community that extends to the sense of community they strive to create and nurture in their classrooms and schools.[1] This conception moves beyond the classroom and school boundaries to embrace the larger, geographic community of families and citizens who care about children and youth. Dynamic teachers enter into a "covenant" with the larger community: "a binding and solemn agreement . . . that represents a value system for living together and forms the basis of decisions and actions" (Sergiovanni, 1992, p. 73). A covenant with the community is grounded in a "shared commitment to ideas, to issues, to values, to goals" (de Pree, 1989, p. 12), and is founded on two basic moral principles: justice and beneficence.

The moral principle of justice is defined as treating equally and respecting the integrity of individuals; the principle of beneficence means that the welfare of the community—the school—is of highest concern. If a school and its wider community accept these principles, then every individual—student, parent, teacher, administrator—"is viewed as an interdependent member of the school as covenantal community and that every action taken in the school must seek to advance the welfare of this community" (Sergiovanni, 1992, p. 106). This covenant entails a stance of empathetic, positive regard for the Other, whether that Other is a young child, a parent, a local shopkeeper, or a colleague.

In describing the "virtuous school," founded on covenantal relationships and grounded in moral principles, Sergiovanni (1992) notes that in such schools,

> parents, teachers, community and school are partners, with reciprocal and interdependent rights to participate and benefit and with obligations to support and assist. It is recognized that the school needs the advice and support of parents if its work in teaching and learning is to be meaningful and effective. By the same token, parents need the advice and support of the school if their work in parenting is to be meaningful and effective. (p. 113)

To this we add the wider community, with its needs and demands and concerns for students and for the school as a central social organization of the community.

Dynamic teachers, then, think of community as a set of relationships: Community is how teachers relate to one another, to students, to parents and family members, to local shopkeepers. And community is a location: the geographic locale that surrounds the school and comprises various groups of people and organizations and agencies. Moreover, dynamic teachers blur the boundaries between classroom and school, school and community, personal and professional; they do not erect artificial demarcation lines. They work with the sure sense that what enriches them personally and professionally will enrich their classroom. They believe that the "outside world" offers substantial resources for them and their students to explore and holds a set of obligations and responsibilities. This world includes their own personal experiences, as well as the experiences of families and other members of the immediate community.

Dynamic teachers are able to relate to this outside world because they bear a stance of humility in the face of knowledge. Dynamic teachers do not construe themselves primarily as information givers; although they bring a body of knowledge to their students, they become co-learners along with the students, as shown in Chapter 5. The enterprise of teaching and learning is no longer about answers; it is about questions. Dynamic teachers have shaken off the burden of having to "know" everything—they present themselves as knowledgeable but real, fallible human beings who no longer play the "I question, you answer" games endemic to classrooms of the past. Their teaching models inquiry. As they teach, they show that students are experts about their own thinking and their own experiences. They enter into a true dialogue with their students that, as Witherell and Noddings (1991) note, is "open; that is, conclusions are not held to be absolute by any party at the outset. The search for enlightenment, responsible choice, perspective, or means to solve a problem is mutual" (p. 7).

The corollary to this stance of humility is that dynamic teachers reach out and invite the resources and experiences of others into their classrooms and search for ways to honor their obligation and responsibility to reciprocate. Within the school, they draw on the expertise of others to enrich their learning environments. They choose not to operate in the egg-crate model of schooling of the past. Although constrained by walls and schedules (which can be frustrating, as Maggie felt), they seek ways to minimize the distancing such structures create. Thus they work with other adults and students in the school to vitalize their vision for learning. The art teacher, for example, becomes a partner in extending and deepening learning about wallpaper in frontier towns. Similarly, the gym teacher could teach games of the mid-1800s.

Dynamic teachers look outside the school as well, feeling a strong sense of reciprocal responsibility to five distinct groups:

- The local business community
- Agencies within the community
- Families representing all the students these teachers serve
- Families of individual children
- Members of various advocacy groups

Each group has resources that dynamic teachers draw on to create more authentic learning environments for children, and each group has legitimate claims on the school, given a relationship of some parity. But dynamic teachers do not slavishly hold to a zero-sum notion of parity: They believe that reciprocity with important external groups is tallied incrementally over the long run. Thus they feel no moral obligation to return resource for resource; rather, they believe that, over time, their commitments to the larger community are being honored.

The Business Community

Dynamic teachers use their own personal and professional experiences to enrich the classroom, drawing on resources they learn about and capitalize on. They are "opportunistic" in the best sense of the word: They seize opportunities that present themselves to serve their students better. From teachers' stories, we learn that "professional practices are embedded in wider life concerns" (Goodson, 1992, p. 16). Maggie, for example, participates in the district's teachers' association. In that capacity, she has been instrumental in learning about the process of collaborative negotiation, an alternative to traditional contract negotiation practices.

Maggie invited an attorney from the community who has become quite well-known for collaborative negotiations to present a
workshop on the new process. Maggie found his approach congruent with conflict resolution ideas she wanted to try out in her classroom, so she invited him into the classroom to tell about what he
does and engage the students in some role-playing about conflict
over the lot lines in the frontier town. He felt uncomfortable in the
classroom, so he offered instead to work with Maggie to develop
some strategies for collaborative resolution appropriate for the students. Maggie refined these ideas and used them in her classroom
to help work through the disputes that had erupted over space. With
practice, the students were able to implement some of the ideas for
collaboration, and the town began to take shape.

The adopt-a-shop strategy brings merchants into the classroom.
Although Maggie and Don were not fully satisfied with the first visit
by the two shop owners, they believed in the idea and continued to
reflect on and assess ways to enliven the experience for both students
and shop owners. Don's follow-up with Mr. Reilly greatly enlightened
their approach and encouraged them both to take more initiative to
send students out into the community as well as to bring community
members into the classroom.

Because of the success of his visit to the shoe repair shop, Don
decided to visit Zing Pao's shop on his way home another day. He
believed that a conversation in the grocer's own space among fruits
and vegetables could elicit more than a strained discussion in the
school setting. He wanted to explore ways students could reciprocate. Perhaps they could contribute to his recycling program, which
gives support to the nearby homeless shelter.

The local business community also gains from a relationship
with the classroom. Don had been talking with a group of doctors
in a nearby clinic about medicine on the frontier. One happened to
mention that she could sympathize with frontier doctors who
served immigrant settlers who spoke a language other than English.
Her practice had taken on a group of Cambodian and Hmong immi-
grants, and the clinic was having difficulty finding a good translator.
Don suggested that the doctor talk to the Hmong boy and girl in his
class. The result was a class project to translate directions and make
signs for the clinic in the several languages various students in the
class spoke.

Local Agencies

Dynamic teachers concern themselves with more than the academic well-being of their students, establishing collaborative relationships with people from health and social service agencies. Don serves on the school council. Also sitting on the council are parents and a community representative. Through this service, Don has learned about the concerns of students' families and feels he touches the pulse of the community. The community representative on the council is a medical doctor from the local health clinic, a satellite of the large hospital several miles away.

During a break in a council meeting, Don approached Dr. Judith Wang and had a conversation with her about the multiple needs of the school's students and families. Several families received support through the welfare system; others relied on social workers for complex family problems; some participated in job training through the state's comprehensive training program; and yet others had very young children and lacked strong parenting skills.

Dr. Wang and Don had heard of the Family Life Services Centers, recently instituted in Kentucky's schools, and thought the model held great promise for reducing redundancy in service delivery and for integrating complex social services for families and children. They agreed that such a center at the school could be a rich source of support for their community. Excited about the idea, each agreed to contact an agency; they would meet again in 2 weeks to discuss the idea with the rest of the council members.

As Don reflected on this meeting and the initiatives he and Dr. Wang had undertaken, he realized that they would have to demonstrate that the plan for a center like this would be cost effective. The local social service systems had been under increasing pressure to reduce costs. He knew that such a center would entail up-front expenses; he was not sure that it would reduce costs over time. He realized that he needed cost analyses. Perhaps Kentucky had done some.

Families of All Students

Dynamic teachers draw on resources offered by families who are committed to improving schooling for all the students in the school.

These families are a wellspring of support and resource for dynamic teachers. They seek ways to include families more fully in the life of the school, often creating a place for them within the school building.

Activist parents at O'Henry had approached the school council the previous year to discuss the possibility of creating a family room in the school. A reorganization of space within the school was called for, given shifts in enrollment patterns: The kindergartens needed another room, whereas the upper grades were being consolidated. The possibility of a large room for the use of families suddenly opened up. Parents described their need for a place where they could meet, share parenting information, be available to teachers and staff, and be more fully integrated into the school. Several parents spoke about how they liked to come to school but always felt like "visitors"; they wanted a place that was theirs, where they could come and not feel intrusive.

Immediately receptive to the idea, the council decided to allocate the large room across from the kindergartens for their use. A core group of parents then went to work, furnishing the room with a cast-off couch and area rug, used toys for young children to play with while there, and a large box for recycling clothing and other household articles. They obtained a long table and chairs from the cafeteria; this provided a working space adequate for the many projects they envisioned. Pamphlets and brochures from service agencies in the area now are prominently displayed, along with sign-up sheets for projects in process and for suggestions for new projects.

Parents and family members, mostly mothers and small children, frequent the family room and describe it as "their place" in the school building. One mother tells how she now feels she can come to school without a specific classroom purpose: She just stops in when she feels like it, knowing the room is there for her use or relaxation. Her preschooler loves coming to school and feels comfortable with the kindergarten teachers, whom he now knows. She believes that his transition into kindergarten next fall will be smooth, given his comfort in the building.

A grandparent talks about how he feels much more involved in the daily school life of his two grandsons. He often comes to the family room in the morning when he drops off the children and stays, knowing that the teachers will draw him into some classroom activity if they need an extra pair of hands. The other day a kindergarten teacher asked him to read stories to the children every Tuesday and

Thursday. Although his grandsons are older, the grandfather feels welcomed and integrated into the school because of this teacher.

The family room has become an educational resource for the school's families, too. Every other Wednesday evening, parents and family members meet in a study group. This week they are focusing on helping their children with homework. Two teachers are coming to help brainstorm strategies for better communication about homework between the school and home. Parents are eager to help out, but many feel inadequate or unsure about the best role they can play. All are hopeful that this session will result in some practices that can be adopted schoolwide to ensure better communication about homework.

In 2 weeks, the group will begin three meetings devoted to the transition to the middle school for parents of fifth-grade students. Many parents have expressed concern about the more rigid structures and apparent impersonality of the middle school, and want to begin now—in the winter—to establish some mechanisms to ensure their children's successful adaptation to this next level. The counselor and several teachers from the middle school will be involved in these sessions.

Families of Individual Students

Dynamic teachers work closely with the families of individual students. They understand that part of their covenantal relationship with families is to honor parents' knowledge about their own children and to infuse that knowledge into everyday interactions with each child. Although they value any information that helps them understand the children they teach, Maggie and Don sometimes feel overwhelmed by the intimate knowledge they have of a family's struggles. The other facet of this relationship is that the teacher knows another side of the student and, as the expert on teaching, can share that knowledge with the family. This promotes substantial *knowing* about the student, a knowing that flows from family to school and from school to family. This knowing helps both family and school become more supportive, nurturing, and challenging of the student's growth as a member of a caring community.

Meaningful collaboration for the welfare of the individual student and for the school is the touchstone of this relationship, expressing the moral principles of justice and beneficence. As Wagner (quoted in Scott, 1994-1995, p. 2) notes, "There needs to be some kind of moral anchor, first in the family, then in family/school collaborations . . . in terms of universal ethical principles."

Maggie reflected on last year's events with Katie, the girl with substantial developmental delays. Katie had been at O'Henry since preschool and was well-known and loved by the school community. As her delays had become more apparent, however, the school's psychologist had pressed for her to be placed in a private school that specializes in her type of challenges. Katie's teacher last year had reasoned that Katie was falling further and further behind, as her language problems constrained her mastery of basic skills and knowledge; perhaps an outside placement would be best for her. A meeting of the core evaluation team was scheduled for a time when Katie's mother and father could attend.

Swaying the other educators at the meeting, the psychologist presented an impressive argument in favor of the private school. Although extensive testing had not pinpointed Katie's specific challenges, the global assessment of her cognitive skills suggested that Fairhaven, a school in a nearby suburb, could respond to her needs. Katie's parents hesitated, partly convinced by the rather bleak picture the psychologist painted. But they loved O'Henry: Katie knew the school, the other children, the teachers. Her entire educational life had been spent here. Torn and conflicted, the parents confided in Maggie a few days after the meeting.

Maggie felt inadequate to help Katie's parents. She had a profound belief in the inclusion of children with special needs but also respected the parents' rights to make their own decision. Nagging at her was a conversation she had overheard in the teachers' room about how Katie was often plunked in front of the television after school as her mother dozed on the couch. And how Katie's father had not installed the software that had been recommended for Katie into their home computer. Maggie was a bit outraged by this news but tried to set it aside as she listened to the parents' sense of helplessness. She could empathize with the guilt and frustration Katie's parents felt.

As Katie's parents talked, their belief in the school became clearer and clearer. Hearing this, Maggie proposed a plan that would honor their commitment to O'Henry but could also involve them more closely in what the school was trying to do. The school needed their help if Katie was to grow and develop as fully as she could. Another meeting was called, this time with Katie's teacher and aide that year, the parents, and Maggie as an interested colleague.

At the meeting, everyone agreed that an outside placement would be more disruptive for Katie than potentially beneficial. Given that Katie would stay at O'Henry, parents and educators had to agree to a set of mutual obligations that had Katie's best interests at heart. They developed a structure for regular communication. Katie would bring home an activity schedule each week that detailed school *and* home activities to support and nurture her language skills. Home activities included eating dinner with at least one parent rather than at her small table in front of the television; reading storybooks at bedtime; and her parents sharing with her teacher and aide any new interests or unusual events. School activities focused on building a circle of friends for Katie and gradually easing her into independent lunchtime in the cafeteria, in addition to the pedagogical approaches used by her teacher and aide.

As Maggie reflected on Katie's growth thus far this year, she felt pleased and realized that it would probably not have occurred without Katie's parents. Katie now led the class out to recess, basketball firmly in her hands. Her developing large motor skills, as well as her increasing attempts to articulate her ideas and feelings, had been noted by her classmates who, Maggie believed, were enriched by Katie's presence in the classroom. They were more respectful of one another, tolerant of those who needed more time, and willing to adjust their expectations at the basketball hoop.

Advocacy Groups

Dynamic teachers also work closely with various advocacy groups, including parents of children with identified disabilities and bilingual students and people representing other "special interests." Maggie and Don sometimes wish these groups would just fold up shop and become part of the total school community. Although both recognize the need for affinity with those who share a common concern or issue, Don particularly feels they fragment the school rather than foster a shared sense of purpose. Maggie, however, rebuts with the importance of not overlooking the strong feelings and needs of groups advocating for particular children.

Inherent in the principles of justice and beneficence are moral dilemmas, because the obligation to respect the integrity of the individual may at times conflict with the welfare of the group. Such is the tension that exists with advocacy groups. Parents and family members of students who represent particular groups have legitimate rights and responsibilities toward the school that transcend the needs of their own children. The very notion of advocacy for a particular group, however, may preclude a larger vision of the total school community. There are no easy resolutions to this dilemma, as Maggie and Don have learned.

Three years ago, a group at O'Henry, including Maggie and Don, introduced the idea of two-way bilingual classes in the primary grades. They had visited the Vibrant Springs School and had been impressed with the first-grade classes that were a model for two-way bilingual education in the state. Two first-grade classes contained 10 English-speaking and 10 Spanish-speaking children. The children in these mixed language groups spent half the day with an English-speaking teacher and the other half with a Spanish-speaking teacher. The two teachers were more than enthusiastic about the academic progress of their students as well as the general acceptance of both languages and the strong friendships established across language groups. The visiting teachers returned to O'Henry filled with ideas for just such a program.

Presenting this to the council, the teachers ran into unexpected opposition from Mrs. Sanchez, who represented the bilingual parent advisory council. She took the position that the Spanish-speaking students would lose academic ground if they were forced to learn English at the same time that they were establishing a foundation in their native Spanish. She also feared that the benefits of the rich immersion in Latino culture provided by the primary-level bilingual program at their school would be lost. This program heavily involved parents and family members and created a very special minicommunity within the larger school. Mrs. Sanchez and other parents were worried about how very young children would respond to a setting that mixed Spanish and English over the course of a day. Better these young children have 2 or 3 years in the bilingual program before being gradually introduced to the larger school culture. To complicate the situation further, other parents from the same bilingual advocacy group expressed opposing views the following week, strongly endorsing the two-way bilingual concept.

Maggie and Don had not realized how deep these beliefs ran, nor how disassociated some bilingual parents felt from the rest of the school. Once again, they were struck with the range of perspectives on a single issue. Much chagrined, they knew they should have involved Mrs. Sanchez and other parents from the beginning in their exploration of alternative programs. Perhaps if several parents from the advisory council had been able to visit the Vibrant Springs School with them, much of this upset might have been avoided. They realized that they had offended these parents and that they had to reestablish trust, communication, and common purpose.

SUMMARY

Dynamic teachers do build bridges between their classrooms and their external communities. Maggie and Don have shown that this task is not easy. Like many others, they encounter difficult challenges as they strive for this greater connectivity with the community.

One source of these difficulties is that, as communities change, people hold vastly different notions of what is appropriate for teachers to do and what schooling is all about. Some of these notions emerge from people's perceptions of what schools meant to them; others from what is presented in the media; and yet others from their neighbors' experiences. Some notions even grow out of myths about how schooling can help one achieve the American dream.

Dynamic teachers build bridges to the community because they construe the community as part of their professional commitment, not because someone tells them it is the right thing to do. They believe strongly these connections will help enrich the learning of all their students. Community resources bring real life into learning, offering authentic tasks. They provide broader knowledge and experience as well as role models. Dynamic teachers encourage multiple perspectives of the community in their classrooms. They see themselves as one of many sources of knowledge for students. They also accept the responsibility to make these sources accessible, ensuring equality of opportunity to learn.

The connections and constructions of meaning that children make because of these multiple perspectives are often unpredictable. The vision that dynamic teachers have keeps this unpredictability from becoming chaos. Dynamic teachers believe that this apparent cacophony of perspectives does, in fact, enrich their students, helps them better empathize with differing ideas, and fosters a more full understanding of their meanings.

Dynamic teachers think of their classrooms as "nested contexts": The classroom is embedded in a school that immediately serves families. These families are in turn situated within a community. Embracing this larger community are a region, the state, the nation, and ultimately the world. Each context shapes and is shaped by the others, to varying degrees. Rather than the isolated classroom of the past, the learning communities of dynamic teachers embrace and welcome these contexts both as resources to enrich the environment and as "consumers" of their "product." They draw these contexts into the teaching-learning process and respond to the needs and hopes of these contexts. To do this and to perform as true professionals, dynamic teachers must also develop skills as changemakers. We develop this role, perhaps the most difficult one for most teachers, in Chapter 8.

Note

1. This discussion draws heavily from Sergiovanni (1992).

8

The Changemaker

Taking Charge of the Environment

Dynamic teachers become leaders for change, not to escape their classrooms but to create more options within their classrooms. How do they view the world that affects their classrooms? How do they work to change the contexts? What groups do they try to influence? What do they bring to their conversations? Maggie and Don act in a variety of ways to change the worlds that influence their classrooms.

Sonia climbed into Maggie's car as the sun rose in the east. "I'm glad we're getting an early start to the conference," said Maggie. "We've got a 2-hour drive to Capitol City, and I want plenty of time to cover the exhibits before we give our workshop."

"You get so excited about going to these things! It's rubbing off on me—although I don't really know what to expect. Thanks for taking me."

" 'These things' are my life's blood! I get excited because I learn so much every time I go to a conference—the resources, the ideas, the people you meet. I used to think it was enough just to come home with lots of stuff—book samples, lesson ideas . . . now I want to share what I learned. That's why we're doing the workshop today on our frontier town."

"You said I should join the organization. What's in it besides the conference?" asked Sonia.

"The journal keeps you up on the hot topics in the profession. They often have national networks or task forces to work on specific issues. I was selected 2 years ago for the national network on multiage grouping. We've developed a set of guidelines for teachers who want to try alternative groupings. Remember how I introduced a draft to the faculty earlier this year? And Don contributed to the math standards. Associations keep you from burying your head in the sand!" rambled Maggie.

"You're on the union board too, aren't you? How do you do it all?" wondered Sonia.

"I find it harder if I don't do it. I know we are leaving the class with Don today, but I don't do this to get out of the classroom; I do it so I can have more freedom in the classroom. That's my point with the union—I want to see their strength used the right way. I felt good when we got our roles on the site-based management teams defined in the contract."

"Don serves on the local council, doesn't he?" noted Sonia. "I still don't see how either of you have time for it all."

"Oh, we make choices. Don is so involved with the community. He's one of the founders of that 'safe streets' group. Years ago, I did a lot with students. Now, I'm active with the professional associations and the union," Maggie explained. "Different people do different things—Silvia is secretary of the board of the local education foundation; the money they raise helps us do things we could never do otherwise. Judy volunteered for that legislative task force on educational improvement. There's so much to do."

"You said all this activity makes teaching easier. I'm not sure I understand. I seem to have enough to do just planning my lessons.

"Don't think I don't remember those days! But learning from others makes it all easier. And I feel pretty strongly about what 'should be' in school. If I just close my door and wait for it to happen, I may wait forever. Part of my job is to contribute—to help make a change for the better—for education, not just for my students. Sometimes I do things that aren't easy for me to do—like a few years ago when I testified before that legislative committee for inclusion—but how else can we be heard?"

"Well, I know I'm hearing you," declared Sonia. "I didn't quite expect student teaching to be what you and Don have made it for me. You two have turned around my ideas of what teaching is! And this ride alone may be worth as much as the conference. Tell me, are you going to testify before the House committee on school choice?"

*   *   *   *   *

Dynamic teachers are not satisfied with the status quo; they help shape the worlds they work in. They identify and create formal and informal leadership roles and settings for themselves, from working on a school council, to developing curriculum with the school or district, to participating in union activities, to performing community liaison work, to establishing mentoring relationships with other teachers. Given a particular setting or task, these teachers possess and model a mindset for positive leadership; they do not succumb to the sense of powerlessness experienced by so many educators, particularly those who choose isolation as a way of working. Dynamic teachers are changemakers.

Teachers are increasingly being challenged to assume the responsibility of a significant new role that combines the skills of an architect, a catalyst, a diplomat, and an ambassador. The pressure to negotiate the formal system to achieve particular ends for the benefit of all children is growing exponentially. To be successful, teachers find that they must have the fine-tuned skills of a politician: advocating for the needs of all children, regardless of their individual backgrounds and contexts; and negotiating with decision makers, other faculty, and members of the community to convince them of the wisdom of new practices.

Teachers are often called upon not only to represent their programs to the local school boards and members of the community but also to testify to state legislatures about the effects of their efforts, the needs of their students, and the future they envision for their schools. Sometimes the ambassador role is less formal or visible, such as initiating one-on-one conversations about the importance of quality education. These conversations can raise awareness and build commitment. The skills needed to be effective in this role are typically not included in teacher education courses or in-service offerings. The successful teacher consistently finds other means for gaining the experience required to negotiate a system that has seldom respected the voice of the teachers in this more "political" realm.

This role of fomenting change is enacted outside the classroom, but purpose is what differentiates the dynamic teacher as changemaker from other teachers who get involved in teacher leadership activities outside the classroom. The dynamic teacher does not seek to leave teaching or to escape the classroom. Rather, the dynamic teacher knows that he or she must take on roles outside the classroom to be a better teacher in the classroom. The dynamic teacher is not naive. He or she strategically chooses to play these roles as an agent of change.

As changemakers, dynamic teachers draw on specific skills: They organize; they inform; they collaborate and work for collective action; they catalyze; they negotiate; they advocate. They do not start out with all these skills. As they grow into this role, they learn and develop new skills. Because they are lifelong learners, they identify what is needed and seek ways to add skills to their repertoire.

Maggie and Don are teachers who have chosen to play the changemaker. They are at points of their development and careers, whatever their ages, where they want to and can put time and effort into a world beyond themselves (Huberman, 1994). Their involvement can take many forms. They reject the isolation so many of their colleagues accept as a given. Their presence in a discussion, either formal or informal, raises its level; they believe they can make a difference, so they do make a difference.

Ideas and the Political Community

From the perspective of a changemaker, Maggie and Don see society surrounding their classroom as a political community, or "polis," in which ideas are the most powerful medium of exchange and mode of influence (Stone, 1988). Maggie and Don recognize that they must be active contributors to the interactions and alliances that define and drive the actions of the polis. They have come to see the political community as a system, a set of interrelated actions and forces in which they may have circles of influence (Senge, 1990). Within broader areas of public concern exist domains where their specific input may balance or shift choices or behavior. They believe these shifts will affect their classrooms. In the dynamic complexity of the community's system, their interventions are subtle but do make a difference over time.

Because the medium of exchange is ideas, dynamic teachers are well positioned to be changemakers. Their knowledge is their power base. Grounded in their own value base, they can take a stand on important issues. Their skill at framing questions connected to action is instrumental in establishing an inquiry ethic and a commitment to collective problem solving within the community. Darling-Hammond and Snyder (1992) describe such an ethos where the community is continually asking, What is occurring? Why is it happening? Are existing practices accomplishing what we want? Through their questioning and reflection and action, Maggie's and Don's catalyzing energy sets the tone. They may begin the conversation, and they raise its level.

One reason Maggie and Don can be so effective in political conversation is that they operate at high levels of moral and cognitive development. As in their teaching, they are value driven (O'Connell, n.d.; Perry, 1970); they have set their own standards and acknowledge and cope well with conflict, ambiguity, and a complex world (Belenky, Clinchy, Goldberger, & Tarule, 1986; Loevinger, 1977; O'Connell, n.d.); their internally constructed knowledge enables them consciously to choose and enact their commitments (Belenky et al., 1986). Their questions can cut to the basic assumptions of the situation or problem. Their moral and cognitive self-consciousness sets the tone for ethical action.

Circles of Influence

Because they have explicitly chosen to be change agents, dynamic teachers are strategic about their work in the political community. They choose those domains in which they believe their influence can be maximized depending on their individual interest, strengths, needs, and circumstances. They respond to opportunities that present themselves or create opportunities in places where none are obvious. These domains range from as close as within their buildings to as far as national task forces, but they all lie within what the teachers have defined as the political community that affects their teaching. Their purpose is always to make changes for improvement. In each case their choice to become involved is driven by a recognition that to remain silent or inactive is to accept the status quo.

Within the Building

Dynamic teachers engage in a variety of collaborative activities to raise the level of discourse within their schools. For years, Maggie has belonged to a group of teachers that reads and critiques current books on teaching and learning and schools. At first Maggie counted on the group to introduce her to new theory and issues and practices in education. Now she finds she is usually the one who suggests the books and who relates the readings to practice in the O'Henry School. In addition, Maggie served on the design committee for the new school building. She knows that her input directly influenced the learning environment for students, colleagues, and herself: The houses and common space were largely her ideas.

In other schools, we have seen dynamic teachers working in similar groups or teams. Through her long-term membership on the teacher assistance team in her school, Donna feels she has changed the way teachers take responsibility for students' problems.

> Before the team, we tended to refer out any problem. We didn't feel we had enough resources to support us dealing with problem kids in our classrooms. Working in the team, we find those resources. Now it's not "somebody else's" problem! The answers are within ourselves.

For similar reasons, Jerri is an active member of her school's site-based management team. She feels she has helped the team become more than a symbolic advisory group to the principal. Her willingness to share her vision, to investigate what is possible, to make proposals, and to ask hard questions has given the team authority. Jerri notes that, although participation takes energy, fighting the system or even just complaining takes more!

Fran and Robin take part in a lunch discussion group that delves into education topics they are dealing with. They are primary players, pushing the discussions along, adding alternative perspectives, testing out new ideas among colleagues, raising questions, and bringing in an occasional new member. "The lunch group is important to me. It validates me—and I think I am helping to shape this thing everyone's calling the culture of the school," says Fran.

Roger tells us of the times when, as a member of a personnel search committee, he has helped select new faculty. "It matters to me who my colleagues are. Being on the selection committees means that I have some control over whom I'll be working with. There are certain characteristics I look for."

Often, the changemaker relationships within the school are dyadic, with the dynamic teacher sharing his or her wisdom one on one. Just as Maggie and Don have Sonia, many dynamic teachers have student teachers. Carmen often finds herself in conversations with Kelly, her aide, explaining, offering suggestions, encouraging her to finish her studies. Over the years, Cheryl has found herself an informal mentor for new teachers. The dynamic teacher is sharing his or her expertise and values in ways that shape the practice of colleagues.

In the District

The district is the next target for the work of the changemaker. Both Don and Maggie have served on various curriculum framework committees. "The first time I wrote curriculum was when I realized that my ideas about what's important to teach could be part of what other folks did in their classrooms," said Don. "The second time, I made sure that what we wrote wouldn't just sit on a shelf."

Maggie chose to become active in the teachers' association because she wanted to shift the focus of its efforts. She was concerned that the association leadership was only interested in working conditions such as salary and benefits, both areas in which she felt the union had made great gains. She felt the adversarial relationship that existed between the association and the administration and board prevented everyone from working together to make schools better places for all children. If she complained about the association's direction and adversarial position but did not take any leadership role, she would be implicitly supporting them. Like other teachers across the nation, Maggie wanted the association to focus more directly on issues of teaching and learning: goals for students, quality of instruction, class size, professional development opportunities, restructuring the school schedule. Through her association work, she helped establish conditions that would support teachers' involvement with school improvement and school governance (for discussions of the shift in union focus see McClure, 1992, and Rauth, 1990).

In several schools, we have seen dynamic teachers aggressively recruit their superintendents' support and involvement in school change activities. Anita's urging brought her superintendent to the planning sessions of the school improvement team. Anita believes that the superintendent's presence helped legitimize the team while giving him a base from which to argue for the resources necessary to implement the inclusion model the team had chosen. Anita told us,

> I used to think the folks in the central office had all the answers. They don't—but we can help them. Now I realize that Richard [the superintendent] needs our knowledge if he is to fight for the improvements we want. I give him what I know of the classroom, and I expect him to work for the resources we need.

At another school, Cheryl believes that accompaniment of the superintendent and a school board member with the school improvement team at a regional conference on learner-centered schools would pay off in support later.

Jerri represents her district on the citywide staff development committee because experience has taught her that providing opportunities for teachers to learn and grow is the only way to ensure school improvement. Although she recognizes that she is likely to have little influence on this large committee, which is only advisory, she feels she is obligated at least to add her knowledge to the conversation. Her participation provides the potential to advocate for effective and varied staff development opportunities.

In the Profession

Dynamic teachers also seek to change their profession by influencing the way other professionals think about their work. An example is Maggie's realization that attending a conference only to learn was not enough; she began offering workshops as a way to share her discoveries and perspectives about teaching and learning. She said, "I realized that my knowledge, based on my years of practical experience, was worth more if I gave it away. I don't know why I was surprised when other teachers found it so valuable."

Maggie also accepted her principal's nomination for a national association's network on multiage grouping. This group disseminated research-based information on alternative grouping patterns in use. Don contributed to the development of the mathematics standards and thus was part of a small revolution in the teaching of mathematics. In both cases, the teachers' involvement was welcomed because they are so well grounded in their subject matter and pedagogy. Their expertise opened powerful doors for them.

Beyond the immediate practical value of participating in these networks and workshops, new ways to construe their roles and responsibilities are revealed; participation expands teachers' notions of what is possible and provides courage to experiment (Lichtenstein, McLaughlin, & Knudsen, 1992). Professional norms change; collaboration, grounded risk taking, and willingness to be accountable for action becomes accepted—even expected. As teachers work in these professional communities, they find their voices change the way things are.

- Jerri's work on alternative reading programs for urban children led to her school changing from basal readers to trade books.
- Linda's sharing her adaptations of dimensions of learning (Marzano, 1992) increased its use with bilingual teachers.
- Roger's work on multicultural curriculum changed the way his colleagues deal with diversity.
- Cheryl's participation in an assessment network helped identify useful, innovative materials that became part of a resource bank.

These teachers are altering the practices in their profession.

In the Community

Maggie and Don have discovered that the boundaries between the school and its environment are far more permeable than standard practice would indicate. Because they see the community affecting their work inside the school, they choose to move out into the community to influence for the better the interactions that occur. They bring their knowledge to the community; in doing so, they change the way the community looks at the school. Their adopt-a-shop plan for building the frontier town brought several merchants and craftspeople into the classroom.

Mr. Caswell, a local carpenter, helped the children build desks for Sweetwater's schoolhouse. The experience of working with children in a learner-centered classroom dramatically altered Mr. Caswell's view of school:

> Before I came into this class, I didn't think much about school. I don't have any children in school, and my school experience as a kid wasn't too good. Seeing these kids' willingness to work, their perseverance really excited me. I'm not sure I understand exactly what Maggie and Don do to make this so different from the schooling I remember, but now I have a clear image of what can be.

Mr. Caswell was so enthusiastic about the new ways of teaching and learning that he now serves as a community representative on the local school improvement council.

Dynamic teachers also work in the community as changemakers. As Maggie pointed out to Sonia, Don helped organize a "safe streets" campaign, a neighborhood watch when children are going to and from school. The movement began with volunteer bus stop monitors and walking companions and grew to include a downtown watch with merchants keeping an eye on children in town. Don feels good because he sees that the community no longer attributes all problems with kids to the schools: "Both the school and the town care; now both are taking charge!"

Silvia joined the board of a nonprofit community education foundation to keep money flowing into the schools during rough economic times. Like many other communities, theirs suffered when state legislatures capped the amount of money schools and localities could raise through taxes. The foundation began as a source of funding for "frills" such as art and music that were cut from school budgets. Over the years, the foundation became increasingly proactive, creating public dialogue about what is good public education. One year, the foundation granted Don a small amount of money to start a recycling program with his class and to conduct a "green environment" campaign for public awareness. The successful program and campaign resulted in the adoption of a "green environment" curriculum as well as a yearly "Clean-Up and Green-Up" festival in town.

In other schools, we see the connections dynamic teachers make, altering the way local business people interact with individual schools. Lila teaches an after-school sewing class for middle school students in a very poor rural school. The students had been sewing by hand. When parents picked up their children, Lila made a point of asking them in to the classroom to observe the students' progress. One father, who ran the local chamber of commerce, got talking with Lila about having the children sell their work at a flea market near a local tourist attraction. He and Lila arranged for the group to have a booth. Shortly thereafter, the father appeared at the school with five sewing machines donated by the chamber of commerce. He told Lila that he now saw the after-school program as more than just "baby-sitting"; he saw the potential for young people to learn useful skills, and he felt that the community had a responsibility to help make that possibility a reality.

Dynamic teachers' relationships with the larger community affect the school as they alter the way external parties view education and the school and their responsibility to the community's children.

In the Policy Arena

Gaining access to policy-making groups is an emerging strategy dynamic teachers use to change the system. Maggie and Don attend school board meetings regularly; their faces are familiar to board members because they are often on the agenda to describe a program they have initiated or to get permission for a special activity. They often speak during public forums, making their views and positions known. As a result, the board has come to respect and seek out their opinions, and they are usually among those teachers appointed to task forces or committees.

When the state announced the formation of its advisory board for educational reform, both Maggie and Don submitted their names. Although neither was selected, Maggie and Don made a point of contacting a teacher they knew who was selected so they could be sure their voices were heard. Several of the dynamic teachers we know serve on the legislative advisory boards for educational reform in their respective states. Ron feels his contributions to the common core of learning developed in his state has legitimized his beliefs about what children must know. Donna feels her work with the state portfolio adoption has made more common practices that both enhance and better assess student learning.

Others, like Maggie, offer expert testimony at legislative hearings. Maggie has influenced state inclusion policy; Roger's testimony shaped more equitable state funding formulas; Al's testimony to a local board affected its decision to reject a private company's proposal to take over his district's schools; Carmen's information on language acquisition shaped the formulation of a bilingual education policy; Ron's ideas on alternative scheduling contributed to a decision to support selected charter schools.

These teachers' knowledge, played out among school board members and legislators, has shaped education policy that affects the way schools are run and services are delivered.

SUMMARY

Dynamic teachers' relationships within the classroom differ from the traditional relationship between teacher and student. Dynamic teachers recognize that their relationships outside the classroom must also be different. They choose to foment change, focusing strategically on areas where they believe they can have enduring and authentic influence. They see the political nature of society and know that their ideas and knowledge are their bargaining chips in the social community. They use their knowledge to influence change through negotiating, advocating, informing, training, organizing, collaborating, and motivating. Their knowledge and ideas take action that alters the way the public thinks about education. In turn, they influence the shape of practice in schools. They are changemakers.

Epilogue

"The room sure looks empty with the frontier town gone," observed Judy. "I got to where every day I'd stop in to see what was new in 'town.' This really seemed to work for you this year."

"I think so," agreed Maggie. "And I admired the airport your classes built. Things don't always go so well."

"I'll never forget the year you and Sylvia did a woodland," laughed Don. "Some kids thought hamsters would be a nice addition—then someone forgot to latch the cage, and they all got loose. You thought you found them all. Then I remember sitting at a PTO meeting later that week and seeing one peek out from under a chair! Mrs. Mendonca went wild!"

"How could I forget that?" Lee joined in. "She harangued me for not maintaining the school —for 'harboring rodents,' she said! You were there, Judy, so you helped settle things down. I attribute at least one gray hair to that episode! Still, I don't know what I'd do without you four. Your adventures with your classes each year keep the school alive—you set a standard for us all."

The two teams of Maggie and Don and Judy and Sylvia were gathered in Maggie's and Don's common area with their principal, Lee. School had recessed for the summer, and they

were informally reviewing their work that year. Lee was suggesting that the two teams collaborate on a project next year.

"Our groups are both multiage, and they feed into each
other. Why not pilot a broader age span by doing one unit
together? Take something like the airport or the woodland—
either topic is rich enough on the surface for the younger ones
and yet has plenty of room for in-depth exploration. Everyone
could do experiments; the older children's would be more
sophisticated."

"It's certainly worth considering," agreed Maggie. "Let's
talk about it as soon as we have wrapped up this year. Speaking of this year . . . what did you think was best about our
frontier town, Lee? What did you hear?"

For a while they talked about the success of the project.
They identified specific reasons or evidence for saying that
the activities had enhanced children's learning. Lee reported
comments from parents that revealed their support and understanding. "I'm especially pleased with the way you connected with the community. That's something I want to work
on more myself," said Lee. "I think your work was terrific. Still,
there is one area where I think you need some improvement—
your activities for science just weren't good enough."

"What do you mean?" asked Don and Maggie simultaneously.

"What I mean is that I think you may be a little outdated.
You had the students doing pretty much the same old thing.
When you had the class do weather charts for the town and
tried to relate them to the town's operation, I thought you
would get into some of the new information on weather patterns and environmental effect. But you didn't. I was somewhat disappointed. You lost an opportunity there."

The group sat silently for a few minutes. Then Maggie
responded.

"I'm tempted to get defensive and say, 'What do you expect? You want us to do *everything* perfectly? Cut us a little
slack!' But you are right. Speaking for myself, earth science
isn't my forte—and I haven't kept up with anything new in the

field. I thought the unit on weather was OK—but you're saying that OK isn't good enough!"

"I'll buy that assessment," Don joined in, "but telling us it's not good enough isn't good enough to help us! Maggie's right—neither of us has been able to keep up with new knowledge in earth science. So how can we improve? It's a big field. We need some concrete suggestions, some ideas on where to turn."

"Couldn't you arrange for the science director to do some peer coaching, Lee?" suggested Judy. "That helped me when I didn't know what to do when we replaced the basals with trade books several years ago."

"That's not likely to help here. We know strategies; we need more information. And even though he is science director, I'm not certain Gary knows the new stuff well," said Don.

Maggie began thinking aloud. "Right now, I'm not comfortable doing with the earth science material what I know how to do with language arts and social studies and math. I know that material like the back of my hand. I can play with the ideas and make them come alive for children. I don't understand weather and the atmosphere well enough to play with it."

"The district belongs to that regional alliance for math and science teachers. You could join one of the study groups. I'm pretty sure one is on elementary earth science," Lee offered. "I hear that you get introduced to new knowledge— and you get to work with other teachers to create ways to use it in classrooms."

"That might help. It's more like what I need. But what I really want to do is take this course I heard about. It's offered over at State U. This well-known professor who writes a column on the environment in some popular magazine teaches it."

"So why don't you sign up? I'd be happy to approve staff development money for that," Lee encouraged.

"The problem is, it meets during the day, while I'm teaching."

"Oh. That is a problem," agreed Lee. "Still, you give me an idea. I'm willing to ask the superintendent if we can propose this to the school board as a test case for flexible time. You know, he and I have felt that to support teachers' professional development, we need to create new structures and schedules. This provides a perfect place to start. I can't promise anything—except that I will try! If we don't get anywhere, you can still take part in that regional alliance group."

"You know, Lee, it used to hurt when you—or Don—or anyone—told me I needed to work harder at something when I felt I was already working hard. But you—and Don too—do more than criticize. You help me find a way, somehow, to improve what I do. Now, improving is just part of the course!"

Designing Schools for Enhanced Learning

The Regional Laboratory for Educational Improvement of the Northeast and Islands

Designing Schools for Enhanced Learning (DSEL) strives to "capture" and share the processes and knowledge that constitute successful learning environments. DSEL works with and brings together policymakers and educators throughout the region to help them become more reflective about their work and design systems to make schools more learning centered. DSEL staff work closely with a network of 40 schools from throughout the Northeast, Puerto Rico, and the Virgin Islands, at the same time sharing the knowledge gained from this work with other schools and organizations with similar goals.

Working with educators involved in the everyday struggle of school change, DSEL staff promote professional inquiry; support burgeoning school leadership teams and councils; and serve as the all-important outside listener, observer, sounding board, and reflector. In addition, staff write and distribute a variety of publications and hold conferences, focus groups, and working parties on topics such as assessment, community involvement, early childhood, inclusive classrooms, multiage grouping, and challenges faced by urban and rural schools. Rather than create an additional effort, DSEL helps unite other local, state, regional, and national reform efforts committed to improving education systematically.

APPENDIX B

Universal Declaration of Human Rights

Preamble

Whereas recognition of the inherent dignity and of the equal and inalienable rights of all members of the human family is the foundation of freedom, justice and peace in the world.

Whereas disregard and contempt for human rights have resulted in barbarous acts which have outraged the conscience of mankind, and the advent of a world in which human beings shall enjoy freedom of speech and belief and freedom from fear and want has been proclaimed as the highest aspiration of the common people.

Whereas it is essential, if man is not to be compelled to have recourse, as a last resort, to rebellion against tyranny and oppression, that human rights should be protected by the rule of law.

Whereas it is essential to promote the development of friendly relations between nations.

Whereas the peoples of the United Nations have in the Charter reaffirmed their faith in fundamental human rights, in the dignity and worth of the human person and in the equal rights of men and women and have determined to promote social progress and better standards of life in larger freedom.

Whereas Member States have pledged themselves to achieve, in cooperation with the United Nations, the promotion of universal respect for and observance of human rights and fundamental freedoms.

Whereas a common understanding of these rights and freedoms is of the greatest importance for the full realization of this pledge.

This Declaration was adopted and proclaimed by the United Nations General Assembly resolution 217A (III) of December 10, 1948.

Now, therefore, The General Assembly Proclaims this Universal Declaration of Human Rights as a common standard of achievement for all peoples and all nations, to the end that every individual and every organ of society, keeping this Declaration constantly in mind, shall strive by teaching and education to promote respect for these rights and freedoms and by progressive measures, national and international, to secure their universal and effective recognition and observance, both among the peoples of Member States themselves and among the peoples of territories under their jurisdiction.

Article 1

All human beings are born free and equal in dignity and rights. They are endowed with reason and conscience and should act towards one another in a spirit of brotherhood.

Article 2

Everyone is entitled to all the rights and freedoms set forth in this Declaration, without distinction of any kind such as race, colour, sex, language, religion, political or other opinion, national or social origin, property, birth or other status.

Furthermore, no distinction shall be made on the basis of the political, jurisdictional or international status of the country or territory to which a person belongs, whether it be independent, trust, non-self-governing or under any other limitation of sovereignty.

Article 3

Everyone has the right to life, liberty and the security of person.

Article 4

No one shall be held in slavery or servitude; slavery and the slave trade shall be prohibited in all their forms.

Article 5

No one shall be subjected to torture or to cruel, inhuman or degrading treatment or punishment.

Article 6

Everyone has the right to recognition everywhere as a person before the law.

Article 7

All are equal before the law and are entitled without any discrimination to equal protection of the law. All are entitled to equal protection against any discrimination in violation of this Declaration and against any incitement to such discrimination.

Article 8

Everyone has the right to an effective remedy by the competent national tribunals for acts violating the fundamental rights granted him by the constitution or by law.

Article 9

No one shall be subjected to arbitrary arrest, detention or exile.

Article 10

Everyone is entitled in full equality to a fair and public hearing by an independent and impartial tribunal, in the determination of his rights and obligations and of any criminal charge against him.

Article 11

1. Everyone charged with a penal offence has the right to be presumed innocent until proved guilty according to law in a

public trial at which he has had all the guarantees necessary for his defence.

2. No one shall be held guilty of any penal offence on account of any act or omission which did not constitute a penal offence, under national or international law, at the time when it was committed. Nor shall a heavier penalty be imposed than the one that was applicable at the time the penal offence was committed.

Article 12

No one shall be subjected to arbitrary interference with his privacy, family, home or correspondence, nor to attacks upon his honour and reputation. Everyone has the right to the protection of the law against such interference or attacks.

Article 13

1. Everyone has the right to freedom of movement and residence within the borders of each State.
2. Everyone has the right to leave any country including his own, and to return to his country.

Article 14

1. Everyone has the right to seek and to enjoy in other countries asylum from persecution.
2. This right may not be invoked in the case of prosecutions genuinely arising from non-political crimes or from acts contrary to the purposes and principles of the United Nations.

Article 15

1. Everyone has the right to a nationality.
2. No one shall be arbitrarily deprived of his nationality nor denied the right to change his nationality.

Article 16

1. Men and women of full age, without any limitation due to race, nationality or religion, have the right to marry and to found a family. They are entitled to equal rights as to marriage, during marriage and at its dissolution.
2. Marriage shall be entered into only with the free and full consent of the intending spouses.
3. The family is the natural and fundamental group unit of society and is entitled to protection by society and the State.

Article 17

1. Everyone has the right to own property alone as well as in association with others.
2. No one shall be arbitrarily deprived of his property.

Article 18

Everyone has the right to freedom of thought, conscience and religion; this right includes freedom to change his religion or belief, and freedom, either alone or in community with others and in public or private, to manifest his religion or belief in teaching, practice, worship and observance.

Article 19

Everyone has the right to freedom of opinion and expression; this right includes freedom to hold opinions without interference and to seek, receive and impart information and ideas through any media and regardless of frontiers.

Article 20

1. Everyone has the right to freedom of peaceful assembly and association.
2. No one may be compelled to belong to an association.

Article 21

1. Everyone has the right to take part in the government of his country, directly or through freely chosen representatives.
2. Everyone has the right of equal access to public service in his country.
3. The will of the people shall be the basis of the authority of government; this will shall be expressed in periodic and genuine elections which shall be by universal and equal suffrage and shall be held by secret vote or by equivalent free voting procedures.

Article 22

Everyone, as a member of society, has the right to social security and is entitled to realization, through national effort and international cooperation and in accordance with the organization and resources of each State, of the economic, social and cultural rights indispensable for his dignity and the free development of his personality.

Article 23

1. Everyone has the right to work, to free choice of employment, to just and favourable conditions of work and to protection against unemployment.
2. Everyone, without any discrimination, has the right to equal pay for equal work.
3. Everyone who works has the right to just and favourable remuneration ensuring for himself and for his family an existence worthy of human dignity, and supplemented, if necessary, by other means of social protection.
4. Everyone has the right to form and to join trade unions for the protection of his interests.

Article 24

Everyone has the right to rest and leisure, including reasonable limitations of working hours and periodic holidays with pay.

Article 25

1. Everyone has the right to a standard of living adequate for the health and well-being of himself and of his family, including food, clothing, housing and medical care and necessary social services, and the right to security in the event of unemployment, sickness, disability, widowhood, old age or other lack of livelihood in circumstances beyond his control.

2. Motherhood and childhood are entitled to special care and assistance. All children, whether born in or out of wedlock, shall enjoy the same social protection.

Article 26

1. Everyone has the right to education. Education shall be free, at least in the elementary and fundamental stages. Elementary education shall be compulsory. Technical and professional education shall be made generally available and higher education shall be equally accessible to all on the basis of merit.

2. Education shall be directed to the full development of the human personality and to the strengthening of respect for human rights and fundamental freedoms. It shall promote understanding, tolerance and friendship among all nations, racial or religious groups, and shall further the activities of the United Nations for the maintenance of peace.

3. Parents have a prior right to choose the kind of education that shall be given to their children.

Article 27

1. Everyone has the right freely to participate in the cultural life of the community, to enjoy the arts and to share in scientific advancement and its benefits.

2. Everyone has the right to the protection of the moral and material interests resulting from any scientific, literary or artistic production of which he is the author.

Article 28

Everyone is entitled to a social and international order in which the rights and freedoms set forth in this Declaration can be fully realized.

Article 29

1. Everyone has duties to the community in which alone the free and full development of his personality is possible.
2. In the exercise of his rights and freedoms, everyone shall be subject only to such limitations as are determined by law solely for the purpose of securing due recognition and respect for the rights and freedoms of others and of meeting the just requirements of morality, public order and the general welfare in a democratic society.
3. These rights and freedoms may in no case be exercised contrary to the purposes and principles of the United Nations.

Article 30

Nothing in this Declaration may be interpreted as implying for any State, group or person any right to engage in any activity or to perform any act aimed at the destruction of any of the rights and freedoms set forth herein.

References

Argyris, C., & Schon, D. (1978). *Theory in practice: Increasing professional effectiveness.* San Francisco: Jossey-Bass.

Astuto, T. A., Clark, D. L., Read, A., McGree, K., & Pelton Fernandez, L. D. (1994). *Roots of reform: Challenging the assumptions that control change in education.* Bloomington, IN: Phi Delta Kappa Educational Foundation.

Ball, D. H. (1993). With an eye on the mathematical horizon: Dilemmas of teaching elementary school mathematics. *Elementary School Journal, 93*(4), 373-397.

Bamberger, J., & Duckworth, E., with Gray, J., & Lampert, M. (1982). *Analysis of data from an experiment in teacher development* (Mimeo). Cambridge: Massachusetts Institute of Technology.

Barth, R. S. (1986). On sheep and goats and school reform. *Phi Delta Kappan, 69*(4), 293-296.

Beane, J. A. (1990). *A middle school curriculum: From rhetoric to reality.* Columbus, OH: National Middle School Association.

Beck, L. (1991). *Reclaiming educational administration as a caring profession.* Unpublished doctoral dissertation, Vanderbilt University, Nashville, TN.

Becker, H. J., & Epstein, J. L. (1982). Parent involvement: A study of teacher practices. *Elementary School Journal, 83*(2), 85-102.

Belenky, M. F., Clinchy, B. M., Goldberger, N. R., & Tarule, J. M. (1986). *Women's ways of knowing: The development of self, voice, and mind.* New York: Basic Books.

Bloom, B. S. (1964). *Taxonomy of educational objectives* (Vol. 1). New York: D. McKay.

Bransford, J. D. (1991). *Reflections on a decade of research on thinking.* Paper presented at the Conference on Cognition and School Leadership, Nashville, TN.

Brooks, J. G., & Brooks, M. G. (1993). *The case for constructivist classrooms.* Alexandria, VA: Association for Supervision and Curriculum Development.

Bruner, J. (1985). Vygotsky: A historical and conceptual perspective. In J. Wertsh (Ed.), *Culture, communication, and cognition: Vygotskian perspectives* (pp. 21-34). Cambridge, UK: Cambridge University Press.

Bucci, J., & Rallis, S. F. (1979). Establishing boundaries. *Opening Education for Children and Youth, 6(2).*

Caine, R. N., & Caine, G. (1991). *Teaching and the human brain.* Alexandria, VA: Association for Supervision and Curriculum Development.

Clark, D. L., Lotto, L. S., & McCarthy, M. M. (1980). Factors associated with success in urban elementary schools. *Phi Delta Kappan, 61,* 467-470.

Clift, R., Veal, M. L., Johnson, M., & Holland, P. (1990). Restructuring teacher education through collaborative action research. *Journal of Teacher Education, 41(2),* 52-62.

Cobb, P. (1994). Where is the mind? Constructivist and sociocultural perspectives on mathematical development. *Educational Researcher, 23(7),* 13-20.

Cohen, D. K. (1988). *Teaching practice: Plus ça change . . .* (Issue Paper 88-3). East Lansing: Michigan State University, National Center for Research on Teaching.

Cooley, V. E. (1993). Tips for implementing a student assistance program. *NASSP Bulletin, 6(549),* 10-17.

Criscoe, J. (1995). *Continuities and discontinuities in home and school expectations for children.* Manuscript in preparation, Vanderbilt University, Nashville, TN.

Crowson, R. L., & Boyd, W. L. (1992). *Coordinated services for children: Designing arks for storms and seas unknown.* Philadelphia, PA: National Center for Education in the Inner Cities, Temple University.

Cummings, T. G. (1981). Designing effective work groups. In P. C. Nystrom & W. H. Starbuck (Eds.), *Handbook of organizational design* (Vol. 2), (pp. 250-271). London: Oxford University Press.

Cunningham, L. L. (1990). Educational leadership and administration: Retrospective and prospective views. In B. Mitchell & L. L. Cunningham (Eds.), *Educational leadership and changing contexts of families, communities, and schools* (pp. 1-18). Chicago: University of Chicago Press.

Darling-Hammond, L. (1988a). Accountability in teacher professionalism. *American Educator, 12*(4), 8-13.

Darling-Hammond, L. (1988b). Policy and professionalism. In A. Lieberman (Ed.), *Building a professional culture in schools* (pp. 55-77). New York: Teachers College Press.

Darling-Hammond, L., & Snyder, J. (1992). Reframing accountability: Creating learner-centered schools. In A. Lieberman (Ed.), *The changing contexts of teaching, The 91st yearbook of the National Society for the Study of Education* (pp. 11-36). Chicago: University of Chicago Press.

de Pree, M. (1989). *Leadership is an art.* Garden City: Doubleday.

Devaney, K., & Sykes, G. (1988). Making the case for professionalism. In A. Lieberman (Ed.), *Building a professional culture in schools* (pp. 3-22). New York: Teachers College Press.

Dewey, J. (1966). *Democracy and education.* New York: Free Press.

Doyle, W. (1983). Academic work. *Review of Educational Research, 52*(2), 159-200.

Driver, R., Asoko, H., Leach, J., Mortimer, E., & Scott, P. (1994). Constructing scientific knowledge in the classroom. *Educational Researcher, 32*(7), 5-12.

Duckworth, E. (1986). Teaching as research. *Harvard Educational Review, 55*(4), 481-495.

Duckworth, E. (1987). *"The having of wonderful ideas" and other essays on teaching and learning.* New York: Teachers College Press.

Eisner, E. W. (1991). *The enlightened eye: Qualitative inquiry and the enhancement of educational practice.* New York: Macmillan.

Fenema, E., Carpenter, T. P., Franche, M. C., & Carey, D. A. (1992). Learning to use children's mathematics' thinking: A case study. In P. C. Matthew (Ed.), *School, mathematics, and the world of reality* (pp. 93-117). Needham Heights, MA: Allyn & Bacon.

Fosnot, C. T. (1993). Rethinking science education: A defense of Piagetian constructivism. *Journal for Research on Science Teaching, 30*(9), 1189-1201.

Freire, P. (1970). *Pedagogy of the oppressed.* New York: Seabury.

Fullan, M. (1993). *Change forces.* London: Falmer Press.

Gardner, H. (1985). *Frames of mind: The theory of multiple intelligences.* New York: Basic Books.

Garrison, J. (1994). Realism, Deweyan pragmatism, and educational research. *Educational Researcher, 23*(1), 5-14.

Goldring, E. B., & Rallis, S. F. (1993). *Principals of dynamic schools: Taking charge of change.* Newbury Park, CA: Corwin.

Goodman, K. S. (1994). Standards, NOT! *Education Week, 14*(1), 39, 41.

Goodson, I. F. (1992). Studying teachers' lives: An emergent field of inquiry. In I. F. Goodson (Ed.), *Studying teachers' lives* (pp. 1-17). New York: Teachers College Press.

Gregory, T. B., & Smith, G. R. (1987). *High schools as communities: The small school reconsidered.* Bloomington, IN: Phi Delta Kappa Educational Foundation.

Grossman, P. L., & Richert, A. E. (1986, March). *Unacknowledged knowledge growth: A re-examination of the effects of teacher education.* Paper presented at the Annual Meeting of the American Educational Research Association, San Francisco.

Hargreaves, A. (1994). *Changing teachers, changing times.* New York: Teachers College Press.

Hoover-Dempsey, K. V., Bassler, O. C., & Brissie, J. S. (1987). Parent involvement: Contributions of teacher efficacy, school socioeconomic status, and other school characteristics. *American Educational Research Journal, 24*(3), 417-435.

Howard, J. (1991, November). *Keynote address.* First annual conference on Designing Learner Centered Schools, Saratoga Springs, NY.

Huberman, M. (1994). *The lives of teachers.* New York: Teachers College Press.

Jackson, P. W. (1986). *The practice of teaching.* New York: Teachers College Press.

James, W. (1918). *Pragmatism and the meaning of truth.* Cambridge, MA: Harvard University Press.

Kerr, S., & Slocum, J. W., Jr. (1981). Controlling the performance of people in organizations. In P. C. Nystrom & W. H. Starbuck (Eds.), *Handbook of organizational design* (Vol. 2), (pp. 116-134). London: Oxford University Press.

Kohlberg, L. (1969). Stage and sequence: The cognitive-developmental approach to socialization. In D. A. Goslin (Ed.), *Handbook of socialization theory and research* (pp. 7-168). Chicago: Rand McNally.

Kolb, D. (1984). *Experiential learning: Experience as the source of learning and development.* Englewood Cliffs, NJ: Prentice Hall.

Lichtenstein, G., McLaughlin, M. W., & Knudsen, J. (1992). Teacher empowerment and professional knowledge. In A. Lieberman (Ed.), *The changing contexts of teaching, The 91st yearbook of the National Society for the Study of Education* (pp. 37-58). Chicago: University of Chicago Press.

Loevinger, J. (1977). *Ego development.* San Francisco: Jossey-Bass.

Loucks-Horsley, S. (1995). Professional development and the learner-centered school. In S. F. Rallis & G. H. Harvey (Eds.), *Theory into practice: Creating learner centered schools, 34*(4). Columbus: College of Education, Ohio State University.

Macrorie, K. (1984). *Twenty teachers.* New York: Oxford University Press.

Marzano, R. (1992). *A different kind of classroom: Teaching with dimensions of learning.* Alexandria, VA: Association for Supervision and Curriculum Development.

Marzano, R. J., Pickering, D., & McTighe, J. (1993). *Assessing student outcomes: Performance assessment using the Dimensions of Learning Model.* Alexandria, VA: Association for Supervision and Curriculum Development.

McClure, R. M. (1992). A teachers' union revisits its association roots. In A. Lieberman (Ed.), *The changing contexts of teaching, The 91st yearbook of the National Society for the Study of Education* (pp. 79-89). Chicago: University of Chicago Press.

Meyer, J. W., & Rowan, B. (1977). Institutionalized organizations: Formal structure as myth and ceremony. *American Journal of Sociology, 83*(2), 340-363.

Miller, J. L. (1990). *Creating spaces and finding voices: Teachers collaborating for empowerment.* Albany: SUNY Press.

Mirman Owen, J., Cox, P., & Watkins, J. (1994). *Genuine reward: Community inquiry into connecting learning, teaching, and assessing.* Andover, MA: The Regional Laboratory for Educational Improvement of the Northeast and Islands.

Murphy, J. (1991). *Restructuring schools: Capturing and assessing the phenomenon.* New York: Teachers College Press.

Murphy, J., & Hallinger, P. (1984). Policy analysis at the local level: A framework for expanded investigation. *Educational Evaluation and Policy Analysis, 6*(1), 5-13.

National Commission on Excellence in Education. (1983). *A nation at risk: The imperative for educational reform.* Washington, DC: Author.

National Council of Teachers of Mathematics. (1989). *Curriculum and evaluation standards for school mathematics.* Reston, VA: Author.

National Council of Teachers of Mathematics. (1991). *Professional standards for teaching mathematics.* Reston, VA: Author.

O'Connell, E. C. (n.d.). *Developmental changes module.* Andover, MA: The Regional Laboratory for Educational Improvement of the Northeast and Islands. Unpublished manuscript.

Perry, W. G. (1970). *Forms of intellectual and ethical development in the college years.* New York: Holt, Rinehart & Winston.

Phillips, D. C., & Soltis, J. F. (1985). *Perspectives on learning.* New York: Teachers College Press.

Piaget, J. (1970a). Piaget's theory. In P. Mussen (Ed.), *Carmichael's manual of child psychology* (pp. 707-732). New York: John Wiley.

Piaget, J. (1970b). *Genetic epistemology* (E. Duckworth, trans.). New York: Columbia University Press.

Popper, K. R. (1972). *Objective knowledge: An evolutionary approach.* Oxford, UK: Clarendon Press.

Presidential Task Force on Psychology in Education. (1993). *Learner-centered psychological principles: Guidelines for school redesign and reform.* Washington, DC: American Psychological Association and Mid-Continent Regional Educational Laboratory.

Purpel, D. E. (1989). *The moral and spiritual crises in education: A curriculum for justice and compassion in education.* Granby, MA: Bergin & Harvey.

Rallis, S. F. (1988). Room at the top: Conditions for effective school leadership. *Phi Delta Kappan, 69*(9), 643-647.

Rallis, S. F. (1990). Professional teachers and restructured schools: Leadership challenges. In B. Mitchell & L. L. Cunningham (Eds.), *Educational leadership and changing contexts of families, communities, and schools, the 89th yearbook of the National Society for the Study of Education* (pp. 184-209). Chicago: University of Chicago Press.

Rauth, M. (1990). Exploring heresy in collective bargaining and school restructuring. *Phi Delta Kappan, 71*(10), 781-784, 788-789.

Reich, R. B. (1992). *The work of nations.* New York: Random House.

Richardson, V. (1994). Teacher inquiry as professional staff development. In S. Hollingsworth & H. Sockett (Eds.), *Teacher research and educational reform, The 93rd yearbook of the National Society for the*

Study of Education (pp. 186-203). Chicago: University of Chicago Press.

Rivzi, F. (1990). Horizontal accountability. In J. D. Chapman (Ed.), *School-based decision-making and management* (pp. 199-324). London: Falmer Press.

Schon, D. A. (1991). *The reflective turn.* New York: Teachers College Press.

Schwarz, P. (1994). Needed: School-set standards. *Education Week, 14*(12), 34, 44.

Scott, B. D. (1994-1995). Parents: A call to action. *Roaring Thunder: Developments on the American educational horizon, 1*(3), 1-2.

Senge, P. (1990). *The fifth discipline.* New York: Doubleday Currency.

Sergiovanni, T. J. (1989). Value-driven schools: The amoeba theory. In H. J. Walberg & J. J. Lane (Eds.), *Organizing for learning: Toward the 21st century* (pp. 31-40). Reston, VA: National Association of Secondary School Principals.

Sergiovanni, T. J. (1992). *Building community in schools.* San Francisco: Jossey-Bass.

Sergiovanni, T. J. (1994). *Moral leadership: Getting to the heart of school improvement.* San Francisco: Jossey-Bass.

Shulman, L. (1987). Knowledge and teaching: Foundation of the new reform. *Harvard Educational Review, 55*(2), 1-22.

Sizer, T. R. (1984). *Horace's compromise: The dilemma of the American high school.* Boston: Houghton Mifflin.

Solomon, Y. (1989). *The practice of mathematics.* London: Routledge.

Soltis, J. (1994). The new teacher. In S. Hollingsworth & H. Sockett (Eds.), *Teacher research and educational reform, The 93rd yearbook of the National Society for the Study of Education* (pp. 245-260). Chicago: University of Chicago Press.

Sparks, D. (1994). A paradigm shift in staff development. *Journal of Staff Development, 15*(4), 26-29.

Starratt, R. J. (1991). Building an ethical school: A theory for practice in educational leadership. *Educational Administration Quarterly, 27*(2), 185-202.

Staub, E. (1979). *Positive social behavior and morality* (Vol. 1). New York: Academic Press.

Stone, D. A. (1988). *Policy paradox and political reason.* New York: Harper Collins.

Torney-Purta, J. V. (1984). Human rights. In N. J. Graves, O. J. Dunlop, & J. V. Torney-Purta (Eds.), *Teaching for international understanding, peace, and human rights* (pp. 59-84). Paris: UNESCO.

Uhl, S., Perez-Selles, M., & Rallis, S. (1995, April). *Defining moments: Teachers talk about becoming student centered.* Paper presented at the Annual Meeting of the American Educational Research Association, San Francisco.

Von Glasersfeld, E. (1992). Constructivism reconstructed: A reply to Suchting. *Science and Education, 1*(4), 379-384.

Vygotsky, L. S. (1978). *Mind in society: The development of higher psychological processes.* Cambridge, MA: Harvard University Press.

Witherell, C., & Noddings, N. (1991). Prologue: An invitation to our readers. In C. Witherell & N. Noddings (Eds.), *Stories lives tell: Narrative and dialogue in education* (pp. 1-12). New York: Teachers College Press.

Index

CORWIN
PRESS

The Corwin Press logo—a raven striding across an open book—represents the happy union og courage and learning. We are a professional-level publisher of books and journals for K-12 educatiors, and we are committed to creating and providing resources that embody these qualities. Corwin's motto is "Success for All Learners."

Printed in the United States
5690